PLANTS & GARDENS

BROOKLYN BOTANIC GARDEN RECORD

Indoor Gardening

1987

Brooklyn Botanic Garden

PLANTS & GARDENS
BROOKLYN BOTANIC GARDEN RECORD

Indoor Gardening

Vol. 43   1987   No. 1

CONTENTS

Cover Photograph by Elvin McDonald
Forced Bulbs: Hint of Spring

Plants and Gardens, Brooklyn Botanic Garden Record (ISSN 0362-5850) is published quarterly at 1000 Washington Ave., Brooklyn, N.Y. 11225, by the **Brooklyn Botanic Garden, Inc.** Second-class-postage paid at Brooklyn, N.Y., and at additional mailing offices. Subscription included in Botanic Garden membership dues ($20.00 per year), which includes newsletters, announcements and plant dividends.

foreword

People have become accustomed to living with plants—not only at home but in the workplace. Plants provide texture, contrast, color, and according to recent studies, some even improve the quality of the air we breathe.

The spectrum of candidates for indoor growing has widened. In *Plants & Gardens News,* Vol. 2, No. 1 a research report is quoted which indicates that many temperate-zone trees and shrubs grow well indoors. This study opens the door to mind-boggling possibilities. A yew (*Taxus* x *media* 'Hicksii') may grow not only in the garden, but in the living room.

Plant trends change with the times. Here at BBG the Auxiliary holds a semiannual plant sale. It has been noted that sales are on the rise for indoor plants that flower.

Charles Marden Fitch, Guest Editor of *Indoor Gardening,* has photographed and collected plants all over the world. Within these pages are photos of some familiar plants in their native habitats and some not so familiar. He has also collected a superior group of contributors to write on their special areas of expertise.

We hope you will be inspired to try growing plants that you have not known before, that those plants will prosper and your enjoyment be beyond measure.

Barbara B. Pesch
Editor

This photograph shows three small foliage plants for terrariums in their true size. At left Poly-stichum tsus-simense, center is Hedera helix 'Itsy Bitsy', at right trailing Helxine soleirolii (Baby's Tears).

Right: Calathea *sp. on humus of the forest floor in the Peruvian Amazon.*

Below: *The jungle has several different layers of plant growth as you can see in this unique view of a tangled Salvadoran tropical forest. Plants from the lower layers will grow well with less light than the high perched orchids or certain sun-loving bromeliads. Plant hunters are still finding new treasures for your houseplant growing pleasure.*

The World of Indoor Plants

A photo essay by Charles Marden Fitch

The plants we enjoy indoors are those that adapt to our conditions. Favorite indoor plants thrive with moderate temperatures, medium levels of humidity, and light intensities gardeners can provide without too much effort or added expense.

Throughout the world plant species and selected cultivars are treasured as living art. These welcome companions fill a need in gardeners' lives by offering beauty beyond borders—needing no translation to appreciate. These photographs show plants in their native habitats around the world.

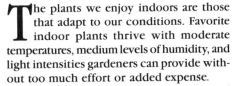

Charles Marden Fitch, horticulturist, photographer, and international media specialist, frequently travels to study plants in tropical habitats. His recent publications include All About Orchids, *and a laser disc containing over 2,000 color photographs of exotic plants around the world.*

Peperomia japonica *thrives on coral rock along the coast in Tahiti. In terrariums peperomias can grow well in lava rock chunks or elsewhere with good drainage.*

Top Left: Platycerium coronarium *and* Polypodium *sp. on a rubber tree growing in central Malaysia.*

Bottom Left: *Tropical jungle plants in Thailand: seen here are ferns and* Pellionia daveauana, *a popular ornamental plant grown indoors around the world. Pellionias are creeping plants well suited to warm humid conditions and low light. The species seen here at left, center and right, is appreciated for its bronze foliage with metallic center stripe.*

Above: Sansevieria ehrenbergi *growing in the dry habitat of Tanzania with Rock Hyrax.*

Below: *Growing epiphytically, these ferns and peperomias grow with roots in humus accumulations and moss on a tree trunk in Costa Rica. High humidity and mists at the 2,200 meter altitude keep plants plump, even during the dry season.*

Above: *Charles Marden Fitch, guest editor, examines bromeliad* Tillandsia multicaulis *growing on a Central American mountain slope. Passing clouds provide high humidity.*

Aroids

James B. Watson

Of the over 2,000 species of aroids, only a fraction are grown as houseplants. Many come from the tropics where they grow as understory plants (thus adapted to low light levels) making them durable houseplants. There are other genera and species for those who seek unusual plants to grow in their apartment, home, or greenhouse. Aroids can also be moved outdoors onto the patio or balcony during the summer.

Members of the aroid family are often difficult to identify because of the diversity in leaf shapes and patterns, but they all possess the same floral structure. Aroid flowers are tiny and packed onto a fleshy spike, called a *spadix*. The spadix is accompanied by a modified leaf called a *spathe*. Spathes are usually green or white, but some are other colors. The bright orange flowering anthuriums popular in flower arrangements are well-known aroids.

Philodendrons, dieffenbachias, caladiums, and some other aroids contain crystals of calcium oxalate in their stems and tubers. When chewed, these crystals puncture mucous membranes, causing swelling and skin irritation. Parents may want to keep young children away from aroids with such irritating crystals. The pain caused by calcium oxalate crystals can be soothed by placing a teaspoon of sugar in the mouth, or with cool liquids or lime juice. Gardeners taking cuttings or dividing tubers can wear plastic gloves to protect their skin.

Opposite: Monstera friedrichsthalii *climbs a tree trunk near Palenque, Mexico.*

James B. Watson is a member of the International Aroid Society, and has served on its Board of Directors. He works at Fairchild Tropical Garden in Miami, Florida.

Culture

Aroids are not demanding culturally, making them good choices for busy people who love plants, but don't want to spend time caring for them. A sampler for beginners includes: *Aglaonema, Dieffenbachia, Philodendron,* Pothos (*Epipremnum*), *Spathiphyllum,* and *Monstera deliciosa.*

Light. Aroids can be placed next to windows or several feet away. Some will grow in dark places, but they should be moved near a window periodically to encourage new growth. *Aglaonema, Dieffenbachia,* Pothos, and *Spathiphyllum* grow satisfactorily in the light commonly found in offices and stores. Aroids in greenhouses need shading during the summer. Acclimate them to brighter light before placing them outdoors during the summer. Keep the leaves looking their best by removing dust with a damp cloth.

Several aroids are small enough to grow under fluorescent lights. Place them 12 to 18 inches from the tubes. Some aroids to grow under lights are: *Anthurium scherzerianum* (pigtail flower), *Anthurium amnicola* (also called *A. lilacina*), and compact hybrids, such as *A.* 'Lady Jane,' *Aglaonema costatum, A. rotundum, Alocasia bullata, A.* 'Fantasy,' *Caladium humboldtii, Philodendron grazilae, Spathiphyllum wallisii* and *S. floribundum variegatum.*

Water. Keep soil moist, not wet or bone dry.

Humidity. Philodendrons, monsteras, and aglaonemas tolerate 20 to 30% humidity, but they prefer 50% or higher. A general rule is that aroids with thick leaves tolerate lower humidity than those with thin leaves.

Fertilizer. Fertilize once a month with 20-20-20 or a similar plant food. Feed plants in dark areas less frequently during the winter.

Temperature. They require warm temperatures to flourish. Day temperatures of 70 to 80 °F with a 5 ° drop at night are ideal. Some aroids show leaf damage at temperatures below 55 °, although a few tolerate temperatures down to 45 ° for a short period.

Soil. Use a well-drained mix, such as equal parts peat moss, perlite, and pine bark mini-nuggets, or add perlite or shredded tree fern to a basic mix for houseplants.

Containers. Select a container made of clay, plastic, or wood. Styrofoam containers are adequate for small aroids, but they are not heavy enough to hold large plants upright. Grow trailing aroids in tree fern, plastic, clay, or wooden slat baskets, or wire baskets lined with moistened sphagnum moss. Vining aroids can be trained on cedar stakes or other supports.

Pests. Aroids are relatively pest-free but aphids and mealybugs can infest new growth or the petioles (leaf stalks) where they join the main stem. Control pests by spraying them with soapy water (Basic H or a gentle, organic based soap).

Water plants early in the day and make sure there is good air circulation around the plants to prevent fungus problems. Remove damaged leaves and inflorescences to keep aroids healthy and looking their best.

Propagation

Aroids may be propagated by air layering, cuttings, division, tubers, and seed. Commercial growers also propagate aroids through tissue culture, but this method is not appropriate for the home grower.

Seeds. Aroids rarely set seed in the home and greenhouse. Since the seeds are short-lived many mail order firms do not sell them. However, new hybrids are grown from seed, and sometimes seeds of new species are received from the jungle.

Separate the seeds from the pulp of the berry. Germinate the seeds on sphagnum moss, a mixture of equal parts peat moss and perlite, or a prepared mix, such as Jiffy-mix. Provide warmth, a shady but lighted area, and moisture. Fertilize seedlings with quarter strength plant food every two weeks. When they develop several leaves, pot them in community pots or individual containers in a porous mix.

Air-layer. Air-layering a stem reduces transplant shock when it is removed. Air-layer the leggy stems of slow-growing aroids, such as the velvet-leaved anthuriums, some philodendrons, dieffenbachias, and *Homalomena rubescens.* Place a handful of moistened sphagnum moss around the stem. Cover it with plastic tied at the top and bottom, or with aluminum foil crumpled around the stem. Cut the stem after roots grow into the moss.

Cuttings. Philodendrons, pothos, Chinese evergreens, and syngoniums are among the many aroids that can be propagated by tip cuttings. Shoots at the base of aglaonemas, anthuriums, and philodendrons can also be cut and rooted. Place cuttings in a damp mix of equal parts peat moss and perlite.

Division. When aroids fill a pot, unpot the plant and cut it into several pieces. Divide plants in the spring or summer.

Tubers. Alocasias and caladiums grow from rhizomes and tubers. New ones are produced, often in the summer. These can be dug and repotted when the parent plant is dormant or in active growth.

Directory of Aroids

This list includes aroids commonly grown as houseplants and some rarer collectors' items. The botanical name, common name, and methods of vegetative propagation are given for each genus.

Code for method of propagation: A = air-layer, C = cutting, D = division, T = tuber R = rhizome..

Aglaonema. (Chinese evergreen. C, D.) These herbs are native to areas where it rains for half of the year and then is dry. Aglaonemas are perfect for gardeners who water irregularly. They also tolerate low humidity and light levels.

A. modestum has erect stems and pointed, glossy green leaves. The leaves of *A.* 'Silver Queen,' *A.* 'Silver King,' and other cultivars are green variegated with silver or other shades of green. The leaves may be rigid or lax, with flat or wavy margins.

The following aglaonemas require high humidity and more care. *A. pictum* has dull, velvety leaves which are bluish-green with patches of silver-grey. It grows one to two feet tall. *A. pictum* var. *tricolor* has pink leaf stalks

This Anthurium gracile *plant was grown from seed collected by the Guest Editor, Charles Marden Fitch in the Peruvian Amazon area. The berries are deep orange.*

and two shades of grey in its leaves.

A. rotundum and *A. costatum* grow eight inches tall. Grow them under lights, in dish gardens and terrariums. The thick, succulent leaves of *A. rotundum* are coppery green with pink veins above and wine-red below. *A. costatum* has thinner, larger leaves—green speckled white. Several cultivars show variability in the amount of variegation.

Alocasia. (Elephant's ear. D, R.) Alocasias require warmth, moisture, and high humidity. In dry atmospheres they may be attacked by spider mites. Look for tiny red spiders and white webs on the lower leaf surface.

A. 'Portora,' *A.* 'Calodora,' and *A.* 'Novodora,' are large evergreens with scalloped-edged leaves. Use them in garden rooms or greenhouses. A smaller species is *A. cucullata*

which has pointed leaves eight inches long. *A. bullata* is eight inches tall with heavily textured leaves. It is also sold as 'Hawaii,' and 'Quilted Dreams.'

Many alcoasias have shiny leaves in shades of green, grey and purple. There may be contrasting white or silver veins, and purple or red undersides. Several of these are *A.* x *amazonica, A. lowii, A. sanderiana,* and *A. watsoniana.* The 12-inch scalloped leaves of *A. cuprea* are metallic copper. The cultivar 'Blackie' has larger leaves with more black color. These fancy-leaved alocasias go dormant in the winter if temperatures drop below 60°.

The one-foot-long leaves of *A. micholitziana* are velvety green with contrasting white veins. *A.* 'Green Velvet' has leaves twice as large and with showier veins.

Anthurium. (A, C, D.) Flowering anthuriums are now available in colors other than orange and red—pink, mauve, green, and brown. Some have speckled spathes and others have double or triple spathes. Indoors, anthuriums require bright, diffuse light and high humidity to flower. Outdoors, in the tropics of Hawaii and Jamaica, growers provide up to 70% shade from hot tropical sun, to improve spathe color.

Compact flowering anthuriums may be grown under lights. Try *A. amnicola* (also sold as *A. lilacina,* lilac spathes, eucalyptus odor), and *A.* 'Lady Jane' (rose-pink spathes). *A. scherzerianum* has a red spathe and yellow spadix. Its common name pigtail flower refers to the coiled spadix.

Many anthuriums are grown as foliage plants. Several have velvety leaves with glistening white veins. *A. clarinervium* is compact. Three collector's items with larger and fewer leaves are *A. forgetii, A. magnificum,* and *A. warocqueanum.* Many hybrids are also available. Air-layer plants with leggy stems.

Strap-leaved anthuriums have leaves that resemble belts. Grow them in hanging baskets. Strap-leaved anthuriums, and those with velvet leaves, will not grow well at temperatures below 60°.

Several strap-leaved species are available. *A. gracile* has 12-inch-long leaves. *A. bakeri* has longer leaves and sets clusters of red berries. *A. wendlingeri* has leaves 30 to 40 inches

long. Its spadix is coiled. *A. vittariifolium* is similar.

Philodendron *'Spider' with its much-cut leaves appears delicate and feathery.*

Many anthuriums have heart-shaped leaves. *A. brownii* and *A. watermaliense* can be grown as houseplants. *A. radicans* is a ground cover or basket plant with stiff, bubbly leaves.

Anthurium veitchii is the most striking foliage anthurium. Its pendant three-foot-leaves are rippled, causing light to be reflected from the glossy, dark green surface.

Some anthuriums have lobed leaves. *A. polyschistum* is a delicate vine. *A. podophyllum* is a shrub.

Bird's-nest anthuriums have rosettes of leaves. They grow in low or bright light and will tolerate low humidity. Many have green leaves and are sold unidentified. *A. guayanum* (also sold as *A. jenmanii*) has dark maroon new leaves. The leaves of *A. superbum* are dark green above and purple below.

Caladium. (Angel-wings, mother-in-law plant, elephant's ear plant. D, T, R.) Caladiums are grown for their showy leaves.

C. humboldtii has two-inch green leaves spotted white. This miniature can be grown under light or in a terrarium.

Large, fancy-leaved caladiums are sold by name through nurseries and catalogs. Many have been developed since hybridizing began in France in the late 1900s. The leaves may be green with red, purple, pink, or white veins or speckling. Some have white leaves with green veins or a pink blush.

Grow them as container plants, in window boxes, or on the patio. The tubers begin to grow in February or March. Plant one or several to a pot and provide moisture, warm temperatures, and bright light for healthy growth. When the foliage dies down in the autumn, withhold water and let the tubers remain dormant for the winter.

C. lindenii, sometimes sold as *Xanthosoma lindenii,* is an evergreen with striped leaves that resemble a zebra. Propagate it by dividing the rhizomes.

Dieffenbachia. (Dumb cane, dumb plant, mother-in-law's tongue plant. A, C.) Dieffenbachias are popular in offices, stores, and dark corners of the home. They can also be grown in bright light near windows. As the stems grow it is natural for the lower leaves to yellow and die. Cut these leaves off.

When there is a tall stem with only a few leaves at the top, it can be cut back. Cut the tip into a stem cutting with several leaves. Root it in a mix of equal parts peat moss and perlite, or in a glass with a few inches of water. Cut the long stem into segments two or three inches long and lay each piece horizontally in the mix. Each will sprout and grow into a new plant. The stem left in the pot will also grow into a new plant.

Many cultivars with variegated leaves are sold in grocery stores and nurseries. The common ones are 'Rudolph Roehrs,' 'Exotica,' and 'Tropic Snow.'

Epipremnum. (Pothos, hunter's robe, taro vine, devil's ivy. C.) Small pots and hanging baskets of pothos have juvenile leaves which are two or three inches long. Plants grown on trees in the tropics bear adult leaves which are two feet long with slits. The leaves of *E. aureum* are green with yellow markings. *E.* 'Marble Queen,' a cultivar with pure white markings, is less vigorous.

Homalomena. (A,C.) These succulent herbs require warmth and high humidity to grow successfully. *H. rubescens* can be kept low or grown to four feet. Its smooth, round, dark green leaves are borne on red petioles. The red spathes, which look like short cigars, are clustered along the stem. Many homalomenas are sold unidentified.

Monstera. (Window-leaf. C.) Monsteras are evergreen vines which can be grown on stakes or against a wall. Stems in hanging baskets rarely trail.

M. deliciosa is a common houseplant with two common names, ceriman and swiss-cheese plant. Several forms are cultivated. The leaves may be 12 to 30 inches long. One cultivar has variegated leaves. *M. deliciosa* tolerates low light and humidity, and will grow under many cultural conditions.

Philodendron (A, C.)Philodendrons fill many interior niches. Many are large shrubs and vines which have different growth habits. Most philodendrons tolerate low humidity and light, but do better with bright light and 40 to 50% humidity.

Self-heading philodendrons have a rosette of leaves on a short stem. *P. selloum* has deeply lobed leaves. *P. speciosum* has triangular leaves. A compact hybrid two feet in diameter is *P.* 'Pluto.'

Most philodendrons are vines, suitable for hanging baskets. Some have reddish leaves. Vining philodendrons with long stems can be grown on stakes or other supports. *P. scandens,* a common houseplant, has heart-shaped leaves five inches long. The leaves of *P. squamiferum* have irregular wedges cut out of them. Its stiff stem is bristly. The leaves of *P.* 'Spider' are cut into many long, narrow, stiff segments. *P. grazielae* is a slow growing miniature with round leaves.

Several philodendrons have variegated leaves. The velvety leaves of *P. gloriosum* are green with white veins. *P. mamei* has quilted green leaves overlaid with silvery-grey variegation.

Rhektophyllum. (C,D.) *Rhektophyllum mirabile* is an evergreen with heart-shaped leaves. They are green with patches of white between the veins. Propagate by division or cutting off the stolons and rooting them like cuttings.

Schismatoglottis. (Drop-tongue. D.) These compact herbs have variegated leaves. Some are speckled or banded green or cream, while others have a burnished look. They require moist soil, high humidity, and temperatures above 60°F. Small species can be grown under lights. Many are sold unidentified.

Philodendron *'Red Princess' requires support. The bold leaves open red and change to green.*

Spathicarpa. (D.) *S. sagittifolia* is grown for its curious inflorescence. The spathes resemble small blades of grass. It grows to eight inches in height. Plant it in small pots or terrariums, or grow it under lights.

Spathiphyllum. (Spathe flower, madonna lily. D.) Spathiphyllums have strap-shaped green leaves. The spathes are usually white, rarely green or pink. These evergreens require plenty of water. Drooping leaves signal they need water. Divide plants every few years to keep them healthy.

Common varieties are *S. clevelandii* and *S.* 'Mauna Loa.' *S.* 'Mauna Loa St. Mary' is five feet tall with white spathes the size of dinner plates. *S.* 'Mauna Loa Supreme' is similar, but more compact.

Several compact spathiphyllums can be grown on tables or the windowsill. *S. wallisii* grows 14 inches tall with glossy, wavy-edged

Monstera deliciosa has deeply cut, mature leaves while the new ones are solid. Sturdy roots shoot out along the stem seeking support for the upward growing leaves.

leaves. 'Svend Nielsen' has wider, glossier leaves.

Spathiphyllum floribundum variegatum has quilted leaves variegated dark and light green. It grows eight inches tall. Its tiny, narrow spathes are white. Grow it in a dish garden, terrarium, or under lights.

Syngonium. (C.) *Syngonium* vines grow well on stakes or totems. As a stem grows, the leaf shape changes from a small arrowhead-shaped leaf to one with several lobes. The leaves may be green or variegated white, yellow, or silver. *S. podophyllum* is commonly called nephthytis, African evergreen, and arrowhead vine. Its leaves are green. The cultivar 'Albovirens' has white and green leaves.

Learning More
Additional information on aroids is available through the International Aroid Society, P.O. Box 43-1853, South Miami, Florida 33143 U.S.A. *Aroideana,* an illustrated journal, is published quarterly by the Society.

Common Names of Aroids

African Evergreen: *Syngonium podophyllum*
Angel-wings: *Caladium*
Arrowhead vine: *Syngonium podophyllum*
Ceriman: *Monstera deliciosa*
Chinese evergreen: *Agloanema*
Devil's ivy: *Epipremnum*
Drop-tongue: *Schismatoglottis*
Dumb cane: *Dieffenbachia*
Dumb plant: *Dieffenbachia*
Elephant's ear: *Alocasia, Caladium*
Hunter's robe: *Epipremnum*
Madonna Lily: *Spathiphyllum*
Mother-in-law plant: *Caladium*
Mother-in-law's tongue plant: *Dieffenbachia*
Nephthytis: *Syngonium podophyllum*
Pigtail flower: *Anthurium scherzerianum*
Pothos: *Epipremnum*
Spathe flower: *Spathiphyllum*
Swiss-cheese plant: *Monstera deliciosa*
Taro vine: *Epipremnum*
Window-leaf: *Monstera*

Top-Notch Begonias

Mildred L. Thompson

Tuberous begonia B. '*Maxwelton' performs well in a hanging basket. Moss-lined wire containers are porous and allow for aeration of the roots.*

Photos by E. & M. Thompson

Begonias are a fascinating group of plants. The growth habits of begonias vary greatly. The stems can be erect, or semi-erect, trailing, or climbing. The growth can be of the creeping rhizomatous nature, tuberous, or semituberous. Begonias are divided into eight major groups: canelike, shrublike, thick-stemmed, Semperflorens, rhizomatous,

---

Mildred L. Thompson has been growing and researching in the begonia field for over 25 years. She has written many articles and a definitive book on the subject. Along with her husband she grows over 1600 varieties of begonias.

Rex, tuberous, and trailing/scandent. Within these groups, there are many different leaf shapes and sizes, seemingly endless leaf colors and color patterns, and various sizes of flowers and flower clusters. Most begonias are seasonal bloomers, but some are ever-blooming. The overall size of begonias ranges from miniature to those that grow to 15 feet in height.

This heterogeneity intrigues growers and is undoubtedly the reason that there are over 3,000 different species and cultivars of begonias grown today. This diversity plus the general ease of growing result in an extraordinary group of plants that can be grown and

17

enjoyed in the home, fluorescent light garden, greenhouse, or outdoor garden.

The following cultural guidelines will be appropriate for most begonias. The ideal temperature range for growing begonias is between 58 and 72° F.; they will tolerate much lower and much higher temperatures, but they will not grow at their best. All begonias require plenty of light and/or sunlight in varying degrees to develop into strong, vigorous plants. Grow begonias where the relative humidity is between 40 and 60%. Some unusual begonias with thin foliage may require additional humidity, easily provided in terrariums.*

*Ed. Note: For example the dwarf hybrid "Buttercup" does best in a terrarium.

The potting mix I find successful is: 1 part perlite, 1 part sphagnum peat moss, 1 part soilless mix (under various trade names at garden centers), and 1 part sterile topsoil. Bulb

Begonia 'Preussen' is a shrublike begonia. It is covered throughout the year with vibrant pink flowers on red stalks contrasted by olive-green foliage.

pots make the best containers because begonias are shallow-rooted plants. I prefer to use clay pots or moss-lined wire containers because they are porous and allow aeration of the root system. Good root develpment is the basis of growing specimen plants. Regardless of the type of containers used, repot only when the root system fills the container, and then move only to the next size container.

Proper watering practices are essential for the long lasting health of the plant. When the surface of the soil is dry to touch (not "bone dry"), soak the mix thoroughly until water comes out of the drainage hole. If saucers must be used, allow the water to drain after watering, and then remove the saucer. Overwatering promotes root rot and the loss of leaves, especially the lower ones.

A regular schedule of fertilizing is imperative not only for vigor, but also for the beauty of the plant — good leaf and flower coloring. A complete fertilizer, preferably the liquid type, should be used every three weeks during the active growing season, and every six to eight weeks during the winter months if the begonias are grown within the ideal temperature range and in plenty of light and/or sunlight. If the begonias are in a dormant or semidormant state, do not fertilize until active growing resumes.

In the following section I have selected eight easy-to-grow begonias, one from each of the eight major groups. With each, I have included some of the special needs for that particular group of begonias.

B. 'Tom Ment', a spectacular canelike begonia, has been a favorite among begonia growers ever since it was introduced by Tom Mentelos in 1973. It is a result of crossing two floriferous begonias, 'Di-Erna' and 'Orange Rubra'. It has large glossy deep green leaves highlighted with large silver spots sprinkled over the upper surface. The deep red undersurface of the leaves adds further color. The margins of the leaves are wavy and slightly cut. Many bamboolike stems develop at the base of the plant, and tend to grow in a graceful semipendulous fashion; staking is seldom necessary. *B.* 'Tom Ment' grows into a full plant in a relatively short period of time. Large pendulous clusters of mandarin orange flowers adorn this begonia throughout the year. It reaches two to three feet at maturity.

There are a few uncomplicated guidelines to follow for this begonia, and other canelike begonias. It is crucial to provide at least four to six hours of sunlight daily for the maximum flowering. Characteristically, canelike begonias are somewhat bare at the base of the plant; nevertheless, when the lower leaves of canelike begonias fall, it is usually because the plants have been overwatered. Many canelike begonias, especially those over three feet tall, need staking in order to get a truly symmetrical shape. In late fall, prune the old woody stems by cutting them back to the third or fourth node; this causes new basal shoots to develop thereby making the plant fuller.

B. 'Preussen' is a popular and easy-to-grow shrublike begonia that is believed to have originated in Germany. It is a compact, bushy plant that sends up many basal shoots, and the thin green main stems are branched. The numerous small, dark olive-green leaves measure about three inches by two inches and, occasionally, the leaves are highlighted with small silver spots; the undersurface of the leaves is tinted purplish-red. The red leaf stems are short which adds to the compact appearance of the plant. Throughout the year, 'Preussen' is covered with large, pendulous many-flowered clusters of vibrant, medium pink flowers that contrast with the red flower stalks and olive-green foliage. This plant grows to about two feet tall at maturity.

Like many of the small-leaved shrublike begonias, 'Preussen' is lovely when grown in a hanging container with stems cascading over the sides while others grow erectly. This type of begonia never needs staking. To keep small-leaved shrublike begonias compact, pinch some of the growing tips periodically and remove any of the older woody stems to allow new growth to develop. To ensure blooming for most of the year, provide abundant sunlight and/or filtered sunlight.

B. 'Perle de Lorraine' is an exquisite winter-blooming thick-stemmed begonia developed in 1901 by Victor Lemoine, a commercial grower in France. It has glossy medium green leaves marbled with chocolate; the undersurface of the leaves is a paler green with maroon marbling. Branching along the main stems creates a bushy plant. From February through April the plant is covered with numerous clusters of soft pink flowers. At maturity 'Perle de Lorraine' is two to three feet tall.

It is essential to provide plenty of sunlight summer through April. Overpotting will accentuate its tendency towards leggy growth so it is best to allow the plant to become slightly rootbound before repotting. 'Perle de Lorraine' will be most attractive if it is grown with the main stems staked and side branches allowed to grow in a graceful pendulous fashion. All thick-stemmed begonias need staking even though, in most cases, the stems are stout and thick enough to support their own weight. Staking will ensure stately erect growth which is one of the outstanding characteristics of this particular group.

B. 'Charm', a striking Semperflorens begonia, was developed in 1948 as a chance seedling of a mutation. It was introduced by

Logee's Greenhouses. The variegated foliage is the most captivating feature of this cultivar; the medium green leaves are splashed with white and yellow. If it is grown in direct sunlight, the leaves will be edged with a deep pink. This low-growing plant is naturally compact because it develops many basal shoots, and it branches along the stems. Pink single flowers are abundant throughout the year. 'Charm' makes a sensational colorful basket plant in all seasons.

Most variegated Semperflorens begonias need protection from direct sunlight particularly during the summer; 'Charm' is an exception. It will be much more attractive if it is grown in lightly filtered sunlight or in a few hours of direct sunlight. Semperflorens begonias need periodic pinching of the growing tips to remain full through all stages of growth.

B. 'Oliver Twist', an exceptional rhizomatous cultivar, was developed in 1978 by Logee's Greenhouses as a result of crossing 'Madame Queen' and B. carrieae, a Mexican species. The most irresistible feature of this begonia is the foliage, medium-sized leaves are ruffled, crested, and highlighted with short white hairs around the leaf margins. The satiny, bronze-green leaves are accented with light bronze-green along the red-spotted veins. The plant is compact with leaves close together. Clusters of pink flowers rise above the foliage in the spring.

Provide sunlight during the late fall to early spring so that the plant will bloom to its full potential. During the summer months the sun's rays must be filtered to prevent fading of the foliage. Most rhizomatous begonias bloom in winter and early spring. It is important not to get water on the leaves, especially those with crested leaves, because this will cause rotting.

Use clay bulb pots or moss-lined wire containers for potting all rhizomatous begonias. Repot only when the root system fills the container so that the plant will remain compact. Pinch the growing tips or terminal buds of the rhizomes to increase branching along the rhizomes. Cut back bare portions to where there is foliage. When all the rhizomes near the edge are foliage laden, allow them to spill over the edge. This will result in the spectacular shape which creates a specimen plant.

B. 'Helen Teupel', an exquisite low-growing Rex begonia, was developed in 1928 by Schmeiss in Germany, and has been an easy-to-grow favorite over the years. The leaves are egg-shaped, with wavy margins and pointed lobes — deep garnet blending into a deep green outer band outlined with garnet. The outer half of the leaf is heavily splashed with silver between the main veins. The undersurface of the leaves is mahogany red and dark green. 'Helen Teupel' is a creeping rhizomatous-type Rex begonia with foliage-laden rhizomes spilling over the sides of the container. At maturity the plant forms a ball-like shape, making it especially attractive in a hanging basket.

Rex begonias have flamboyant ornamental foliage. Like most Rex begonias 'Helen Teupel' prefers a higher humidity, over 45%, and a temperature of 65 - 72 °F. Rex begonias should be grown in bright light without direct sunlight except in the early morning or late afternoon. If the plant becomes one-sided, pinch the tips of the rhizomes to force growth in the other direction. This advice applies to all rhizomatous type begonias including rhizomatous Rex types. Avoid overwatering and overpotting.

B. partita, a lacy-looking semituberous species, was originally collected in South Africa in the late 1800's. B. partita did not come to this country until 1978 when a commercial seedsman sent me seeds that had been collected in Natal, South Africa. The plant has small medium green, deeply cut maple-shaped leaves highlighted with red-tinted veins, reddish stems and petioles. It is full and naturally bushy. There is a large semituberous formation at the base of the plant. White flowers adorn this particularly interesting species from spring through the fall. The mature plant is about two feet in height. Be certain never to overwater because the semituberous formation will rot. When it is very humid and cool, this begonia is susceptible to powdery mildew; if this occurs, spray with a fungicide immediately to prevent widespread damage. To maintain a full and bushy plant, pinch the growing tips at fairly regular intervals to induce branching. B. partita prefers to be slightly rootbound, and this feature makes this group of species especially suitable for growing in rock and driftwood plantings. In addition, these semituberous species can be trained into handsome sculptured plants. Their maple-shaped leaves create the appearance of small trees and the semituberous formation adds to the sculpted effect. These tuberous species go into a semidormancy during the winter months if the temperature in the growing area falls below 60°. If this semidormancy occurs, water sparingly and stop fertilizing until active growth starts, (usually when temperatures become higher).

B. solananthera is a beautiful trailing species from Brazil where it was first collected in the mid 1850's. This species has many trailing woody stems about two feet in length with much branching along the stems. The heart-shaped leaves are a rich medium green, about two to three inches long by one and a half to three inches wide. In the winter, the plant is covered with clusters of sparkling white flowers with crimson centers highlighted by the vivid yellow of the anther of the male flower and the style and stigma of the female flower. Each flower cluster has eight to ten flowers which protrude slightly beyond the foliage. The flowers are fragrant.

The long trailing stems enable the plants to be grown beautifully in hanging containers. To insure a compact plant, pinch the growing tips of the newer shoots to induce branching along the stems. Pinching should be started in the early stages and continued through the entire life of the plant. As the plant matures, cut back the old, bare woody stems closest to the basket so that the newer growth can take over. Plenty of winter sunlight is required for this species to bloom abundantly.

I have mentioned above the most important guidelines for growing begonias. With study and experience, each grower will develop a sense of the individual needs of each plant. 🌿

Begonias can be propagated easily from leaf cuttings. This single leaf of B. 'Gay Star' produced a clump of plantlets.

Top: Schlumbergera *'Gold Charm' often flowers in both winter and spring.*

Gymnocalycium mihanovichii *v.* friedrichii *has attractively marked stems with abundant pink flowers.*

Photo by John N. Trager

Succulents for Indoor Growing

John N. Trager

F ew of us live in climates mild enough to grow succulents outdoors. When culti-vated, these plants are therefore usually restricted to conservatories, smaller green-houses, clustered on sunny windowsills, or under artificial light. Conservatories in botan-ical gardens can afford space for some of the more imposing succulents. The average col-lector, however, must make do with much less space. Many succulents oblige with appropri-ately subdued growth or lilliputian propor-tions. Such miniatures are suited to limited space and their exotic forms and remarkable flowers are better appreciated when placed on a shelf or windowsill closer to eye level.

Some succulents are demanding in their cultural requirements and will not achieve their full potential indoors. This is an under-statement for those of us who have labored only to find our treasures smothered with pests or collapsed in a heap of rotten mush.

These and most other problems encoun-tered in growing succulents can be prevented or even cured. By providing certain basic growing conditions and selecting adaptable species, one can raise healthy specimens. Of the 10,000 species of succulents, only about 3% are suitable indoor plants.

While more complete information is avail-able elsewhere, a few basic points about cul-tivation of succulents are worth reviewing.

Light: The limiting factor for growing suc-culents indoors is usually light. Few succu-lents will look their best with less than three or four hours of direct sun a day. Plants grown in less sunny areas should have supplemen-tal light from an artificial source that provides a complete spectrum. The effectiveness of artificial light dissipates quickly with distance from its source. Therefore, succulents must

Crassula 'Buddha's Temple' is grown mostly for its attractive foliage as are other members of this family.

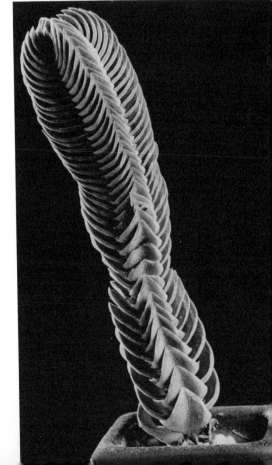

John Trager, Horticulturist of the Desert Gar-den Conservatory at the Huntington Botani-cal Gardens, is a writer, lecturer, and photographer of succulents. His work appears in the "Cactus and Succulent Journal," the "Euphorbia Journal," and the Abbey Garden catalogs.

Aloe bellatula has coral pink bell-shaped flowers. This species has a dwarf growth habit so it is suitable for a three- to four-inch pot.

gen, 5-10% phosphorus and 5-10% potassium) with every watering during the growing season.

Dormancy: Most succulents require a dry, dormant period in winter—water lightly or not at all. Dormant plants don't absorb water and soggy soil may lead to rotting. One unavoidable side effect of this rest period is the natural dieback of roots. As already mentioned, however, an annual or biennial spring repotting and root pruning will take care of this problem and stimulate fresh growth. Cut root ends should be allowed to dry in the open air for several days before repotting or, if potted immediately, not watered for a week or so.

Pest Control:* Another frequently encountered problem resulting from incomplete watering is root mealybug harbored in dry pockets within the rootball. Mealybugs are small, cottony-looking insects which suck plant juices from roots and other parts. Above the soil they are easily removed with a forceful jet of water or a toothpick. Below the soil, root mealybugs must be controlled with a drench of systemic insecticide. One drenching in spring and one in fall will usually keep mealybugs in check.

The only other common pest of some succulents is spider mites. These nearly microscopic arachnids suck juices from the leaves of thin-leaved succulents such as adeniums and occasionally from soft-stemmed cactilike rebutias. The early symptom is minute, yellow flecking on the leaves. Heavy infestation results in a fine webbing over the surface of the leaves which upon examination with a magnifier will be seen to be crawling with the little reddish mites. Rebutias, unfortunately, don't show symptoms until the epidermis becomes irreparably scarred and corky over the entire stem. Commercial miticides are usually quite effective against mites.

*Ed. note: We recommend the conservative approach in controlling pests. Keep plants healthy and clean, inspect often and use insecticidal soap if necessary—not commercial sprays.

be placed at close range (four to six inches) in order to benefit.*

Watering: When actively growing, succulents should be watered thoroughly, then allowed to dry until the soil is barely damp before watering again. Soil moisture below the surface can be determined by probing with a toothpick or the plant's name tag (which is also handy if you can't remember names). If allowed to dry out completely, feeder roots will die. These will harbor rot which may spread to living tissue.

Feeding: Plants grown in low light will require little if any feeding. Periodic repotting will provide enough nutrients as well as the opportunity to inspect roots and prune off any that have died back during the dry winter dormancy period. Plants grown in a brightly lit greenhouse will require regular feeding for optimal growth. The best fertilizer is a dilute solution of low nitrogen fertilizer (¼ strength of a fertilizer with 5-10% nitro-

Succulents for Form and Flowers

These guidelines alone will not ensure success. One must select the right plant for the right place. Indoor growing conditions are

*Editor's Note: See feature *Houseplants Under Lights* on page 82.

usually somewhat different than plants are accustomed to in the wild. Therefore, adaptability is an essential characteristic for indoor succulents. What follows is a brief selection of some of the more interesting succulents, ones which are better adapted than most to growing indoors. They are chosen for their general availability from nurseries specializing in succulents, their reasonable cost (most under $10), adaptability to indoor conditions and their desirability. The last criterion refers to their beauty, intriguing forms or flowers or a combination of these attributes.

Succulents for Form

Caudiciforms: One group of succulents grown for their often bizarre or grotesque forms is the caudiciforms. These plants have unusually thickened, non-green stems or roots. Often the caudex develops underground but can be raised gradually with each

Rhipsalidopsis rosea *is a dwarf epiphytic jungle cactus that bears light pink flowers.*

successive repotting. *Adenium obesum,* for example, develops a marvelous caudex of stem and intertwining roots and has the added attraction of beautiful, pink, bell-shaped flowers. *Fockea edulis* has inconspicuous flowers, but its caudex becomes magnificently obese, covered with a knobby, silvery skin. *Pachypodium lealii* ssp. *saundersii* has smooth, silvery skin, particularly in the new growth, as well as delicate, white pinwheel flowers in the fall.

The succulent ficuses, *Ficus palmeri* and *F. petiolaris,* have green, heart-shaped leaves, with red veins in the latter species. Both have succulent trunks and roots that can be trained over a rock in bonsai fashion. They develop a flaky bark, resembling old, weathered wood with peeling varnish. The weathered effect is even more pronounced in *Cyphostemma juttae* in which the bark peels off in sheets. In seemingly out of place juxtaposition are its large fleshy leaves which are covered with a waxy coating like the "bloom" of a fresh plum. *Senecio tuberosus* has similarly waxy, but much more proportional leaves atop its stems which emerge from knobby, jointed tubers that can be raised to make an interesting miniature bonsai. The caudiciform mass often has natural arches through which one can peer. The roots of *Trichodiadema bulbosum* resemble a cluster of contorted carrots. Its leaves are tipped with starlike clusters of stiff hairs and the plant is further ornamented for several weeks in summer with half-inch magenta flowers.

Some euphorbias have tuberous roots that can be exposed as a caudex. Some, like *E. tortirama* and *E. groenewaldii,* have twisted, corkscrewlike branches as well.

Other Stem Succulents: Other succulents, while not caudiciforms, can also be grown indoors for their exotic stem forms. Many cacti, for example, have pleasingly symmetrical stems, either columnar or globular, and ornamented with intricate spine clusters arranged in rows along ribs or in spirals. *Espostoa lanata* is a columnar cactus with ribbed stems, though these are barely visible as they are densely clothed in a cottony fur produced among the small spines and concealing them. Another white-hairy columnar cactus is *Oreocereus celsianus.* Its hair, however, is coarser and doesn't hide the thick awllike amber-colored spines. While these two white-haired cacti are somewhat different than the better known "Mexican Old Man Cactus," *Cephalocereus senilis,* they are better suited to indoor growing than the "Old Man," which is rather temperamental about overwatering.

Another cylindrical-stemmed cactus grown for its form is *Borzicactus aureispinus,* whose one-inch thick stems are covered with short yellow spination almost furlike in its density. The stems branch from the base and droop, creating a wonderful hanging basket plant for a window where backlighting will show off its beautiful spination. The freely produced, coral-pink flowers are an added bonus to this adaptable cactus.

Globular cacti are either smooth-stemmed or tubercled with the spine clusters born on these raised mounds. *Coryphantha bumamma,* for example, has bold clusters of clawlike, recurved spines surmounting equally bold tubercles.

Many of the euphorbias are superficially similar to the cacti in their vegetative form. *E. polygona* 'Snowflake,' for example, has columnar, ribbed stems with a thick, waxy white epidermis, while *E. obesa* has a globular, striated stem resembling a hot-air balloon in miniature.

A completely different sort of stem form is seen in *Senecio pendula,* the "Inch Worm Plant," which undulates in and out of the soil in a manner reminiscent of its namesake.

Succulents for Foliage: Among the succulents grown primarily for their foliage are several hundred species of the crassula family. The genus *Crassula,* for example, includes *C. falcata* with four-ranked, bladelike, grey-green leaves arranged in propellerlike fashion. This species has been hybridized with many other *Crassula* species resulting in myriad, marvelous foliage forms. Perhaps the choicest of these is the hybrid with *C. mesembryanthemopsis* called *C.* 'Morgans Beauty.' While the brilliant scarlet flower color of *C. falcata* usually washes out when crossed with paler flowered species, this hybrid with the white-flowered *C. mesembryanthemopsis* has resulted in a compact plant with overlapping, sculptured leaves and clusters of bright pink flowers with a honeylike perfume.

Another group that has lent itself to hybridization is the dwarf aloes of Madagascar. *Aloe descoingsii,* with its nearly ever-blooming habit, crossed with a variety of beautiful foliage plants like *A. rauhii* and *A. parvula* has resulted in some floriferous hybrids with beautiful rosettes of leaves and some rather humorous names like *A.* 'Lizard Lips.'

The related haworthias also have decorative rosettes of leaves and are ideal house-plants by virtue of their tolerance for shade. Some like *H. retusa* and its allies have translucent "windows" in the upper surface of the leaves which make them appear as though cast of green glass. Others like *H. nigra* are opaque, with rigid leaves arranged in elegant, three-sided towers, as though sculpted of dark jade.

One of the best euphorbias for foliage is *E. neohumbertii,* which, in addition to its beautifully marked stem, has broad paddle-shaped leaves during spring and summer. It is remarkably shade-tolerant with the leaves growing larger in low light. *Hoya kerrii* has similar, but thicker and heart-shaped leaves that persist the year round.

One group of foliage succulents that has lured many into attempting to grow them are *Lithops* or "Living Stones." Their fused pairs of stonelike leaves come in a remarkable variety of intricate patterns and are replaced by a new pair annually. The rule of thumb in lithops culture is to water only when they begin to shrivel, and then lightly. However, when the new leaves are emerging in winter, they derive all their needed moisture from the old leaves which undergo a natural shrivelling as they are absorbed.

Succulents for Flowers

The ultimate goal of any horticulturist is to have a plant flower. In addition to those flowering species already mentioned, there are many other succulents that flower as well. Their flowers are often all the more remarkable for their contrast to the unusually shaped plants from which they emerge.

Ceropegias, on the other hand, have flowers that are seemingly unreal. These bizarre, ornamented, vaselike structures are designed to attract fly-pollinators as are the notorious "carrion-flowers" like *Stapelia*

Dwarf creeping Sedum dasyphyllum *is grown here in a small bonsai pot. The leaves are glaucous blue.*

nobilis which emit an odor like that of rotting flesh from their six-inch hairy flowers. While *S. nobilis* is not suited as a centerpiece for the dining room table by virtue of its scent, *S. flavopurpurea* has delicate, two-inch, yellow flowers with a sweet, honeylike fragrance. The related huernias have no scent at all to their wonderful array of flowers, some of which (*H. hystrix*) are covered with rasplike teeth. Others, like *H. zebrina,* have a prominent, raised buoylike ring in the center.

Some cacti have nocturnal flowers with a delicious perfume designed to attract moth pollinators. For those collectors who work days and can only enjoy their plants at night, these plants have a special appeal. Among the choicest night-flowering cacti are *Echinopsis subdenudata* and the *Discocactus* species, all with white flowers, and *Arthrocereus rondonianus* which is unusual among night-bloomers for its pink flowers.

Succulents for Indoor Growing

The preceding whirlwind tour of succulents gives only a hint of the remarkable variety of species that can be grown indoors. In the absence of space to discuss and illustrate all the possibilities available to the collector of indoor succulents, the following list will serve as a guideline for future acquisition of other succulents for form and flowers.

□ = caudiciform stem and/or root
■ = desirable for the feature indicated

Plant	Stem	Foliage	Flowers
Adenium obesum	□		■
Agave polyanthiflora		■	
Aloe 'Lizard Lips'		■	■
Aloe albiflora			■
Aloe bellatula			■
Aloe descoingsii		■	■
Aloe haworthioides v. *aurantiaca*		■	■
Aloe parvula		■	
Aloe rauhii		■	■
Aloe rauhii 'Snowflake'		■	■
Aloinopsis schooneesii	□	■	
Arthrocereus rondonianus	■		■
Beaucarnea recurvata	□		
Begonia venosa	■	■	
Borzicactus aureispinus	■		■
Ceropegia species			■
Ceropegia woodii		■	
Clusia rosea		■	
Coryphantha bumamma	■		■
Coryphantha elephantidens	■		■

Plant	Stem	Foliage	Flowers
Coryphantha minima	■		■
Coryphantha missouriensis v. *caespitosus*	■		■
Cotyledon species		■	■
Crassula species		■	■
Cyphostemma juttae	□	■	
Dioscorea species	□	■	
Discocactus species	■		■
Dorstenia species	■	■	
Echeveria species		■	■
Echinopsis subdenudata	■		■
Epiphyllum crenatum 'Chichicastenango'	■		
Epiphyllum hybrids			■
Espostoa lanata	■		
Euphorbia aeruginosa	■		■
Euphorbia clavigera	□		
Euphorbia decaryi		■	
Euphorbia flanaganii	■		
Euphorbia greenwayi (blue form)	■		■
Euphorbia groenewaldii	□		
Euphorbia horrida	■		
Euphorbia leuconeura	■	■	
Euphorbia lophogona	■	■	■
Euphorbia millii v. *imperatae*			■
Euphorbia millii v. *tananarive*			■
Euphorbia neohumbertii	■	■	■
Euphorbia nivulia			
Euphorbia obesa	■		
Euphorbia persistens	□		
Euphorbia polygona 'Snowflake'	■		
Euphorbia pugniformis	■		
Euphorbia squarrosa	□		
Euphorbia suzannae	■		
Euphorbia tortirama	□		
Euphorbia trigona	■		
Euphorbia vigueri v. *ankarafantsiensis*	■	■	■

Plant	Stem	Foliage	Flowers
Ficus palmeri	□		
Ficus petiolaris	□	■	
Fockea edulis	□		
Gasteria species		■	■
Graptopetalum species		■	■
X *Graptoveria* 'Silver Star'		■	
Gymnocalycium species	■		■
Haworthia species		■	
Hoya kerrii		■	
Hoya species		■	■
Huernia species			■
Kalanchoe beharensis	■	■	
Kalanchoe blossfeldiana			
Kalanchoe species		■	
Lithops species			■
X *Lobiviopsis* hybrids	■		■
Mammillaria bocasana	■		■
Mammillaria bombycina	■		■
Mammillaria carrettii	■		■
Mammillaria coahuilensis	□		■
Mammillaria elongata	■		
Mammillaria glassii v. *siberiensis*	■		■
Mammillaria guelzowiana	■		■
Mammillaria haageana (M. elegans)	■		■
Mammillaria hahniana	■		■
Mammillaria humboldtii	■		■
Mammillaria microhelia	■		■
Mammillaria plumosa	■		
Mammillaria saboae v. *haudeana*	■		■
Mammillaria surculosa	■		■
Mammillaria zeilmanniana	■		■
Monadenium coccineum			■
Monadenium magnificum	■	■	

Plant	Stem	Foliage	Flowers
Monadenium montanum v. *rubellum*	□		■
Neochilenia napina	■		■
Notocactus crassigibbus	■		■
Notocactus graessneri	■		■
Notocactus haselbergii	■		■
Notocactus leninghausii	■		■
Notocactus magnificus	■		
Notocactus mammulosus	■		■
Notocactus minimus	■		■
Notocactus ottonis	■		■
Notocactus rechensis	■		■
Notocactus scopa	■		■
Orbea variegata			■
Oreocereus celsianus	■		
Orostachys species		■	■
Pachypodium baronii ssp. *windsori*	□		■
Pachypodium brevicaule	□		■
Pachypodium geayi	■	■	
Pachypodium lameri	■	■	
Pachypodium lealii ssp. *saundersii*	□		■
Pachypodium succulentum	□		■
Piaranthus foetidus v. *purpureus*			■
Rebutia species	■		■
Rhipsalis species	■		■
Sansevieria species		□	
Senecio pendula	□		□
Senecio rowleyanus		□	
Senecio stapeliiformis	□		□
Senecio tuberosus	□		
Stapelia species			■
Tacitus bellus			■
Thelocactus bicolor	■		■
Thelocactus schwarzii	■		■
Trichodiadema bulbosum	□		■
Zamicoculcas zamiifolia		■	

Photo by John N. Trager

Zamioculcas zamiifolia *is a foliage plant that is very tolerant of low light.*

Editor's Note:

The genera and species of cacti occurring in the United States and Canada are defined differently by the authors of various books and papers. Discrepancies like this do not reflect necessarily errors or mistakes in judgment but, rather, differences of opinion concerning policy in classification.

Each botanist attempts to classify plants in a uniform manner, and no system is necessarily "right" or "wrong," provided that the organisms are grouped according to natural relationships and the arrangement is essentially consistent.

There is no comprehensive coverage of the cactus family according to conservative policy. 🌱

—excerpted from The Cacti of the United States and Canada *by Lyman Benson, Stanford University Press, 1982.*

Growing Bromeliads

Adapted from an article by George Kalm-bacher originally published in Plants & Gardens, *Vol. 28 No. 3 1972*

Bromeliads are striking plants and easy to grow indoors. Their flower complexes are eye-catching and will last in good condition for a few months. This long-lasting quality of the beautiful inflorescence and succeeding berries, typical of many bromeliads, is not equaled in any other group of houseplants.

A great proportion of bromeliads grow in trees in the American tropics, the trees serving simply as a perch. Bromeliads do not derive nourishment from their hosts, but manufacture their own life-materials from the abundance of air-borne particles and debris of decaying plant and animal life. So they are not "parasites," and do not bore into their living hosts and suck out vital juices as do parasites.

Living up in the air, perched on other plants epiphytic bromeliads have evolved to a state unique among plants—one that presents two radical changes. The primary purpose of their roots has come to be fundamentally that of support. Their roots are so firmly attached to their hosts as to become practically cemented, and sometimes the area of attachment is very small compared to the size of the plant. The absorptive function of roots has been taken over by small white scales of complicated structure that act like sponges. In some tillandsias, the whole leaf is densely covered with scales. In other bromeliads the scales are in broad bands attractively alternating with greenish bands. In fact, many of the cultivated kinds, even without flowers, are delightful the year around as foliage plants because of markings, spotting, coloring, banding and striping. Foliage attractiveness is further advanced by the introduction of "variegation" to normal leaves. This is the appearance of patches or lines of color which can be shades of yellow or pink or other color, or white. Variegation of bromeliads is usually in longitudinal stripes.

Most of the bromeliads grown as houseplants are of a kind that might be called "water-tanks." These consist of large wide leaves spirally and closely arranged to form elongated receptacles that will hold water without leaking. In some cases water will be further retained in lower leaves that form basal scoops. The sides of the leaves in contact with the water take the place of the absorptive rootlets in other plants, drawing water and dissolved mineral and organic matter necessary for the life-processes of the plants. When applying fertilizer, use the liquid form in the case of the "tank" plants and place in the water of these cups. In nature all sorts of animal and plant debris finds its way into these cups and decays there. When fully broken down, the minute resultants become part of a new cycle of life. This is compost at an aerial level. Some animals live, some die in these tanks. In addition, particles of dust or larger matter, floating in quantity in those tropical areas, fall into the plants' "broth" to supply mineral and organic substances.

Epiphytic bromeliads, like these aechmeas growing on an oak tree outside of Chichen itza's Mayan Temple in Yucatan, require good air circulation around their roots and water in the cups.

George Kalmbacher served for many years as Taxonomist at Brooklyn Botanic Garden. He took a particular interest in cacti, gesneriads and bromeliads.

In the forested tropics with their year-round activity and vast wealth of organic life, ephiphytic plants are a characteristic part of the scene. Not only bromeliads, but their companions—orchids, cacti, ferns—are scattered about, sometimes thickly, other times only lightly.

In strange contrast, there are in desert regions of tropical America, a few kinds of epiphytic bromeliads attached to large cactus plants. And there are also bromeliads that are not epiphytic at all. Some grow on rocks as their regular habitat, some in soil. Of these three types, there are a number that have become unusual subjects for cultivation in homes, greenhouses and outdoors where the climate is warm enough. In fact, outdoor growing, not surprisingly, makes the healthiest plants. If possible, put your bromeliads outdoors when weather is no longer hazardous for them; hang them up in trees or place them under trees where the shade is not dense—and bring them back before cold weather sets in.

Bromeliads have a common system of vegetative multiplication. From seed comes a rosette which will flower in time, but as it grows, it develops low branches or rhizomes, each of which in time develops its own rosette which eventually can be cut off and rooted to become a new plant. Flowering arises from the center of the mature rosette, as a final act, after which it gradually dies. These offsets are commonly called "pups," a term also used in cactus growing. They are usually stocky. Do not cut them off from the mother plant until they are a few inches long.

The most reliable genera for beginners to start with are the aechmeas and billbergias. They want good light, and need only water in their cups. The aechmeas are remarkable for their long lasting flower and berry complexes, sometimes in large panicles. The flowers are small and not nearly as showy as the billbergias, but produce berries without obvious pollination. These solid full berries go through color changes that are highly pleasing, and which altogether last for a few months. One common color range is in the metallic wine-reds with a very glossy finish.

Some species are found in nature that are typically green, but have varieties that are dark red on both sides of the leaf, or some-

Aechmea fasciata *is remarkable for its long-lasting flower and berry complex.*

times only on the underside. The leaves are usually large, and the habit upright and cup-shaped. They require a very porous growing mixture—no soil but plenty of fibre, some inert material such as river gravel, coarse perlite or granite chicken grit, and organic material such as leafmold. It is not necessary to carefully measure the amounts of each, but a heavy proportion of fibre is advisable. In with the mix, scatter Osmocote, a fertilizer consisting of small round beige particles that disintegrate over a long period of time—actually about six months. Among the aechmeas, the following are well-known: *A. chantinii, fasciata, fulgens* and its variety, *discolor, gamosepala, lueddemanniana, miniata* and its variety *discolor, orlandiana, racinae* and *tillandsiodes*. There are also colorful hybrids.

The billbergias require similar culture, but are distinct from the aechmeas in that their tubular flowers are richly colored, larger and very obvious. They come in loose racemes or panicles on long stalks. They put on a show, which, however, lasts only about a week. Since they grow freely and abundantly, clumps develop if undisturbed, and when a number of rosettes in a clump come into flower, it can make a truly grand picture. The very easy and popular *Billbergia nutans* is a great favorite.

Unlike the aechmeas, billbergias do not usually produce seeds in cultivation but hybridize rather easily in nature. Some offspring are not especially distinctive.

Neoregelias and nidulariums should be given the same regimen as the billbergias and aechmeas, except that being softer-leaved, they require a little less light. Both kinds are more open plants, ranging from fairly upright to flattish in habit. They are often considered together because of the colorful areas in the foliage that develop before flowering time, and become more pronounced during the flowering period, which may last for a couple of months or more. In the neoregelias, the flower complex is a large disc in the center, from which single or a few flowers arise at a time over a long period. In the nidulariums, the inflorescence is at the top of a stout stalk with colorful bracts or floral leaves inter-mixed. The flower stalk may not be obvious.

Among the most striking kinds are the vrieseas, but they are delicate to a certain extent. The inflorescences with their bracts, which are often colored rich dark red, enclose individual flowers that bloom one at a time. They are often upright, flattened long spikes. If they are packed tightly in four-inch pots with fern fibre and nothing else, they may not give any trouble, since the drainage is perfect and they will not suffer from water damage, which is probably the great hazard to their successful culture.

There are more tillandsias than any other kinds. Most of them have long, very narrow leaves. A number of tillandsias are attractive for their foliage because of the thick coating of tiny silvery scales. They, like the closely related vrieseas, are very susceptible to water remaining about the roots and plant base, and are best mounted on cork, fern bark or driftwood, with only some fern fibre close around

Guzmania lingulata *has bold red flowers above a rosette of dark green leaves.*

usually have white flowers low in the center of the plant. They do best with the same mixture as the epiphytes if given less water. They do require humid surroundings.

Bromeliads are remarkably free from pests, but scale can be a problem. These roundish, raised and stationary insects can be easily rubbed off when they first appear—if one is on the constant lookout for them.

Miniature Tillandsia ionantha *blushes red in the center as it produces blue flowers in the spring. Its silvery foliage and diminutive rosettes make it attractive at all seasons.*

Vriesia 'Nova' requires at least two square feet of space when fully mature. Olive-green leaves have white bars and flowers are produced on erect inflorescences with green bracts.

the base. They can be securely fastened by putting a little Duco Cement on the wood or bark at the point where the plant is to be attached, and setting the base of the plant in the cement. It takes a short time to dry and then holds the plant in place, where it can proceed to grow a few roots in the manner of tillandsias. They thrive with very little root development. Tillandsias do best in cultivation with misting. Give a good soaking once a week. They do well without fertilizer.

All the above mentioned bromeliads do best in a humid environment. But care must be taken not to overwater—they can withstand dryer conditions than one would expect.

Some Terrestial Bromeliads
Cryptanthus are terrestials, some flattened like stars, and a number have unusual coloring not found in the other genera. They

"Miniature Lady Palms" for Indoor Decoration

Lynn McKamey

The word "palm" often brings to mind the image of towering plants, crowned with feathery thatches of leaves gently swaying near warm tropical shores. While some palms do have coconuts and monkeys, most do not. Over 3,000 different species exist, and several can grow indoors as easily as in their native habitat. A fine example is *Rhapis excelsa,* a small multi-trunk fan palm native to the subtropical regions of China. It is one of the oldest cultivated palms in the world and has been a popular interior plant for over 300 years.

Elegantly graceful and adorned with richly patterned leaves, *Rhapis excelsa* has acquired the common name "Lady Palm." Rare, slow-growing, and long-lived, it is undemanding and prefers low light. Enchanted by these exceptional qualities, the Japanese first began obtaining "Lady Palms" from China in the 17th century as exclusive possessions for Imperial palaces and the highest levels of nobility.

The fame of this esteemed plant soon reached Europe, and *Rhapis excelsa* became one of the first ornamental palms to survive the long, harsh ocean voyages of the 18th century. It was introduced to European conservatories in 1774, and became a classic American parlor palm and garden accent in the 1850's. Many Victorian homes in the South are still surrounded by thick clumps of *Rhapis* over 100 years old. These early cultivated palms were tall 'standard' *Rhapis excelsa,* often growing more than 14 feet in height and attaining immense width. Consequently, it became known as "Large Lady Palm."

All photos by author

Rhapsis excelsa *'Gyokuho' has a short compact growth habit, small, oval leaves and is a slow grower.*

Lynn McKamey is a director of the International Palm Society. She owns Rhapis Gardens in Gregory, Texas, and specializes in developing new varieties of "Miniature Lady Palms."

35

'DARUMA'

28" tall, 5 years old, 7" pot

A classic miniature resembling the large "standard" Rhapis excelsa. Shape is tall and upright.

'KODARUMA'

26" tall, 10 years old, 9" pot

This shortest of all Rhapis has slow, compact growth and numerous offshoots. The ultimate mini-palm.

'TENZAN'

30" tall, 5 years old, 7" pot

A fast growing variety with slender form and long drooping leaves. Quite dramatic.

'KOBAN'

26" tall, 5 years old, 7" pot

Distinctively different with wide, oval leaves and a tall, spreading growth habit. Very popular.

Dwarf Varieties

of

Rhapis excelsa

Common Name:

"MINIATURE LADY PALMS"

'GYOKUHO'

20" tall, 7 years old, 7" pot

A pixie palm with small, oval leaves and a short, bushy growth habit. A favorite of most everyone.

'ZUIKONISHIKI'

18" tall, 9 years old, 6" pot

White and green striped leaves distinguish this as the most vivid variegated.

'ZUIKO-LUTINO'

12" tall, 6 years old, 5" pot

Creamy white leaves with green stripes. From the term "lutino" - white birds with a touch of color.

'KOTOBUKI'

20" tall, 8 years old, 6" pot

White stripes on green leaves make this Lady quite stunning. Tall graceful form with long oval leaves.

As interest in *Rhapis excelsa* continued to expand, Japanese enthusiasts began cultivating new smaller forms of this species, more suited to interior space and their preference for dwarf plants. The shortest, slowest-growing lady palms were selected, cloned and refined to be fully developed specimens only two to four feet tall after decades of growth. Green and variegated sports soon appeared within these miniatures, an unusual occurrence in the palm kingdom! Each new variety exhibited a unique leaf shape, growth habit, and coloration. These outstanding cultivars developed into a splendid group of dwarf *Rhapis excelsa,* collectively called "Miniature Lady Palms."

Over 100 different variegated and green varieties have been named and classified. Though these pedigreed palms can only be propagated by division and remain somewhat scarce, a fascination has developed in the Far East, and dwarf *Rhapis* are in demand as houseplants and fine accompaniment to bonsai. Many Japanese businessmen consider these palms a wise investment and purchase the rarest cultivars as an inflationary hedge. Dwarf *Rhapis excelsa,* a long kept secret of the Orient, was finally discovered by the Western world in the 1960's.

Fortunately for those who love to acquire and grow highly prized plants developed by others, these exquisite palms have now become important additions to interiors and fine plant collections around the globe. The "Lady Palm" charm that captivated those 17th century admirers is still alluring new collectors today. However, modern enthusiasts have the advantage of selecting not only the original standard *Rhapis excelsa,* but also from the vast array of dwarf *Rhapis excelsa* in many green and variegated varieties.

"Lady Palm" Perfection

What virtues could a plant possess to make it popular for more than three centuries? Everyone would like a houseplant which is durable, long-lived, easy to grow and propagate, thrives in low light, and resists insects and disease. Dwarf varieties of *Rhapis excelsa* provide all this, plus being perfectly sized for interior spaces. Those in small pots are excellent table accents, while larger ones make handsome floor specimens.

Of course, nothing is perfect. Price is seemingly the only flaw, since *Rhapis excelsa* are somewhat expensive. Costs are determined by age, size, and rarity. One of the most popular green clones, 'Koban,' ranges in price from $20 for a 14″ tall, three-year-old single-cane division to $150 for a 15-year-old multi-cane specimen three feet in height. Variegated forms are available from under $70 for a 12″ tall, five-year-old 'Zuikonishiki' to the astronomical cost of over $1,000 for a tiny division of the rarest striped form 'Eizannishiki.'

Undemanding Culture of *Rhapis Excelsa*

Symmetry and Growth Habit: *Rhapis* can be easily admired from all sides, since each cane displays a symmetrical leaf swirl. Leaves radiate in six directions, spiraling up the trunk so the sixth leaf is directly above the first. This interesting feature is most noticeable in young single-cane specimens. As the palm slowly adds new offshoots, it transforms into an ever-spreading, bushy clump of foliage and a continuous source of new divisions.

Light and Growth Rate: *Rhapis excelsa* are native to the shaded forest floors of China. Consequently, they easily adapt to low interior light (i.e. enough light to read this handbook without eyestrain). Light intensity is related to growth rate. In low light, a dwarf specimen will basically maintain its present size, slowly adding only one or two inches of height per year, depending on variety. Bright filtered light enables a dwarf *Rhapis excelsa* to grow slightly faster and generate several new offshoots each year. "Lady Palms" should never receive direct sun which may scorch or yellow leaves.

Size: Because *Rhapis* are so slow growing, selection of size is important. If you like to watch small plants grow (slowly) bigger, then purchase a young division 12 inch to 18 inch tall in a five inch or six inch pot. If you prefer larger, fully developed specimens, dwarf varieties can be found in a vast assortment of sizes up to four feet in height, over 20 years old.

Temperature: The temperature range of these versatile palms is 22° to 100° F (−5° to 38°C). They easily adapt to indoor conditions and most shaded tropical or subtropical landscapes. Popular as patio plants in northern regions, they require only a brief period of protection during the coldest winter months. *Rhapis excelsa* is one of the few ornamental palm species to offer such widespread indoor and outdoor use.

Humidity: "Lady Palms" accept dry or humid atmospheres, and do not require constant misting, although they appreciate having their leaves gently washed when dusty.

Watering: Proper watering is the most important requirement for a long-lived, thriving *Rhapis excelsa*. These palms must be thoroughly watered (soaked) and then allowed to become almost dry (not quite wilt). Use a shallow saucer with your palm. Water should be applied so that it slowly drains through the soil and fills the saucer. Empty the saucer if it is still full after several hours. In normal house temperatures and average humidity, most *Rhapis* require watering only once a week or so.

Fertilizer: These slow-growing palms require very little fertilizer. Watch the color of the foliage which should be a deep, rich green. When leaves begin to turn slightly yellow, apply soluble houseplant food or fish emulsion mixed in water at one-fourth the recommended rate listed on the container. Wait several weeks to determine if the palm is "greening;" if not, apply another dose at low rates. *Rhapis* grown indoors seldom require fertilizer more than two or three times a year.

Insects: Scale is the only major pest of this species.

Brown Tips: Light brown "fringe" at the end of leaf segments is typical of *Rhapis* and usually occurs on older, lower leaves. Badly burned leaves are usually caused by over-fertilizing, improper watering, incorrect pot size, or continuous use of alkaline (hard) water. Slightly damaged leaf tips can be trimmed using a pair of "pinking shears."

Pot Size: A "Lady Palm" prefers living in a pot just slightly larger than its root mass. Overpotted palms tend to stay continuously wet and become subject to root rot, whereas underpotted specimens beg for frequent watering and in protest, can push themselves out of the pot (making thorough watering quite a chore!).

Rhapis excelsa *'Tenzan' is a dwarf variety that is an excellent accent for floor or table. The larger specimen is in a twelve-inch pot while the other is an eight-inch pot.*

Soil: *Rhapis* grow best in a well-drained soil rich in humus, such as African violet mix.

Potting: Proper soil density should be firm—not loose, not packed—and allow water to slowly filter through the pot and into the saucer. Soil level should cover all roots and the base of the canes.

Propagation: *Rhapis excelsa* are easily multiplied by division. Gently remove all soil, select an offshoot with enough roots to fill a four inch or larger pot, and separate from the main cane. Spring or early summer is the best time to divide and repot palms.

Life Expectancy: "Lady Palms" can be lifelong companions, since century old specimens are not uncommon. Old cherished *Rhapis* in the Far East are traditionally divided and shared with the next generation.

Questions Most Often Asked

How Delicate Are *Rhapis?* From their graceful leaves to their sturdy roots, *Rhapis excelsa* are tough little plants. Do not be afraid to repot or divide them. They thrive with minimal care, and endure adverse conditions far better than many plants.

Which are the Most Unusual Varieties? Two very different green cultivars come to mind. 'Kodaruma' is the ideal "mini-palm," staying very short and bushy with small leaves and numerous offshoots. It is the slowest growing variety, and may only attain three feet of height after 30 years of age. 'Tenzan,' in perfect contrast, is an unusually fast growing dwarf. This tall, slender variety has large, oval leaves with wide segments. With optimum growing conditions, 'Tenzan' can often exceed five feet of height after several decades of growth.

Culture of Variegateds: Variegated forms generally grow only half as fast as green varieties. They require slightly less light, reduced fertilizer rates, and excellent water quality (lest the leaves burn).

"Miniature Lady Palms" are a delight. Treat yourself to one or start a collection. You will find that each variety has an elegant and unique personality all its own.

Rhapis Relatives

Several different species of *Rhapis* are available, but none are as versatile and adaptable to indoor culture as dwarf varieties of *Rhapis excelsa*. To insure the purchase of a genuine "Miniature Lady Palm," look for a tag listing genus, species, and cultivar, such as *Rhapis excelsa* 'Daruma.' If it does not include a variety name, you might be purchasing one of the following *Rhapis* relatives:

The standard *Rhapis excelsa* ("Large Lady Palm") is becoming more common since seed sources have recently been found in the Far East. All large forms are very similar in appearance and do not offer the distinction of having different named varieties. This familiar big sister of the "Little Ladies" can quickly outgrow interior spaces and is best used as a sizeable, durable palm in tropical and subtropical landscapes.

Rhapis humilus ("Slender Lady Palm") can easily grow to towering heights of 18'. Since it is very difficult to divide and does not produce seed, small container specimens are quite scarce and extremely expensive. This species thrives only in cool, subtropical landscapes and seldom tolerates interior use.

Rhapis subtilis ("Thailand Lady Palm") has only recently acquired its correct botanical name and is often confused with dwarf *Rhapis excelsa* or mistakenly labeled *R. humilis*. This small tropical palm flourishes in warm humid landscapes, but quickly deteriorates in interior environments. It is the only species which cannot be divided, is short-lived, extremely susceptible to spider mites, and must be constantly watered. If it dries, it dies. Abundantly grown from seed imported from Thailand, *R. subtilis* is an inexpensive two to eight foot tall plant, easily recognized by its small leaves with pointed tips. 🖉

Mail Order Source of Miniature Lady Palms:

Rhapis Gardens
100 Rhapis Road P.O.B. 287
Gregory, Texas 78359-0287

Further Reading:

Secret of the Orient, A Lady Palm Reference by Lynn McKamey. A complete guide to Rhapis palms, 52 pages fully illustrated. Available from Rhapis Gardens, 100 Rhapis Road P.O. 287, Gregory, Texas 78359-0287.

Palm Society

The International Palm Society
P.O. Box 368
Lawrence, Kansas 66044

Rhapsis excelsa *'Chiyodazuru' has green leaves which display narrow, evenly spaced stripes. This specimen is 24 inches tall, nine years old, in a seven-inch pot.*

Comparisons of Dwarf Varieties

Uniquely, *Rhapis excelsa* is the only ornamental palm species with named and classified varieties, each having distinctive characteristics. These miniature cultivars provide an exciting choice of exotic forms and textures which are almost unlimited.

(See following pages)

Leaf Shapes and Growth Habits;

Variety Name	Leaf Shape	Growth Habit	Rate of Growth
'Koban'	large, oval leaves	full, spreading	medium
'Daruma'	narrow leaf segments	tall, upright	fast
'Tenzan'	long, oval leaves	tall, slender	very fast
'Kodaruma'	small, twisted leaves	short, bushy	very slow
'Gyokuho'	small, oval leaves	short, compact	slow
'Zuiko-Lutino'	white leaves with green stripes		slow
'Chiyodazuru'	narrow, evenly spaced stripes		medium
'Zuikonishiki'	white and green striped leaves		slow
'Kotobuki'	white stripes on green leaves		fast

Rhapis excelsa *can be easily divided. Spring or early summer is the best time to divide and repot palms.*

Rhapis Palms

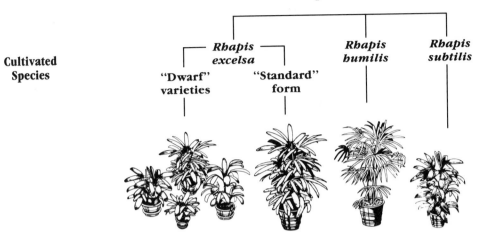

Cultivated Species	Rhapis excelsa		Rhapis humilis	Rhapis subtilis
	"Dwarf" varieties	"Standard" form		

Common Name	Miniature Lady Palms	Large Lady Palm	Slender Lady Palm	Thailand Lady Palm
Origin	China	China	China	Thailand
Variegated Varieties	yes, many	no	yes, a few	no
Canes	thick, sturdy	thick, sturdy	slender, flexible	varies
Leaf Size—Tip Shape	small—blunt	large—blunt	large—pointed	small—pointed
Segments per Leaf	2-10*	6-14*	10-30*	varies
Leaf Thickness	thick	thick	thin	very thin
Maximum Height	4-5 feet	10-14 feet	15-18 feet	6-8 feet
Temperature Range (F)	22° - 100°	22° - 100°	18° - 90°	30° - 90°
Interior Light	low to bright	low to bright	bright filtered	bright filtered
Humidity Range	20%-100%	20%-100%	40%-100%	60%-100%
Long-lived	yes	yes	yes	yes
Propagated by Division	yes	yes	difficult	no
Propagated by Seed	no**	when available**	no, not available	yes
Pests:				
Scale	yes	yes	yes	yes
Spider Mites	seldom	seldom	occasionally	yes, frequently
Landscape Success:				
in California (cool, dry)	excellent	excellent	excellent	poor
in Texas (extremes)	excellent	excellent	poor	poor
in Florida (warm, humid)	excellent	excellent	poor	good
Interior Success	excellent	excellent	fair	poor
Bonsai Success	excellent	too large	too large	too large
Availability	good	good	very scarce	abundant
Price	expensive	expensive	very expensive	moderate
Rating for Overall Use	excellent	excellent	fair	poor

*The number of segments per leaf increases as the palm adds fronds. All species, except for R. subtilis, have a uniform number and width of segments.

**Seed of standard R. excelsa is scarce. Division of dwarf R. excelsa is the only reliable method of perpetuating the selected strains of named varieties.

Gesneriads

For Your

Indoor Garden

Michael A. Riley

Streptocarpus *'Mini Nymph' bears light blue flowers. It is a good candidate for culture under lights.*

The most recognized genus in the Gesneriad family is *Saintpaulia,* the African violet. The modern hybrids are examples of hybridization at its finest. Great interest is attained with the many variegations and variations in leaf and flower color. The symmetry of growth pattern, the abundance of flowers and the ease of culture add up to the perfect houseplant. If there is a secret to growing saintpaulias, it is simply—consistency. Make them happy and keep them that way with consistent water, light, fertilizer and temperature. This approach to growing seems to hold true for many houseplants, particularly those which are indigenous to geographical areas where the plants experience few seasonal changes in temperature and rainfall. Modern aids to this consistency in culture are fluorescent lights, humidifiers and a variety of watering and potting methods such as capillary matting and wick-well containers. Many gesneriads fit into this same cultural pattern and are therefore equally good subjects for the indoor garden.

Episcia is the peacock genus of the gesneriad family. Episcias' quilted leaves offer an infinite variety of subtle metallic colors. The

Michael A. Riley lives in New York, and is a commodities trader, an amateur horticulturist, writer and photographer. He has collected gesneriads in Ecuador and is currently the president of the American Gloxinia and Gesneriad Society.

African violets and related gesneriads line greenhouse benches at the nursery of hybridizer Lyndon Lyon.

growth pattern is similar to a strawberry plant with runners which may be pinched back for a fuller habit or let trail as desired. *Episcia* 'Cleopatra' is one popular plant with pink-variegated foliage and *Episcia* 'Silver Skies' is a perfect miniature with silver leaves outlined in dark chocolate brown. Episcias require good humidity and temperatures above 55°. They grow well in low to moderate light and should be slightly moist all the time.

Streptocarpus, which means twisted seed pod, is an increasingly popular plant with a nice growth habit and beautiful flowers. Modern hybrids such as the Concord and Olympus series are bred for their compact size and floriferousness. The flower is a short flared tube in many shades of white, pink and blue, usually with some striping or a yellow blush in the throat. Some hybrids are almost everblooming and others have somewhat cyclical patterns similar to saintpaulias. When growers get bored with all of those flowers, they can go back to the fascinating species which grow on the steep kloofs or mountainsides of eastern Africa. Some are neat little miniatures such as *Streptocarpus cyanandrus* and others have only a single three-foot leaf which may take two years to grow, flower, set seed and die to start the cycle all over again. *Streptocarpus* should be underpotted and well fertilized for better bloom. Place in an east or west window or under lights and provide good air circulation. They are beautiful in window boxes and are being used as bedding plants in shade and partially shaded locations outdoors.

The popularity of gesneriads began with the florist's gloxinia or *Sinningia speciosa*. Its interest has never waned as a commercial pot plant, but the hobbyist has found the large Belgian hybrids to be somewhat demanding in conditions other than in the high light and humidity of a greenhouse. One strain of *S. speciosa* which has been repeatedly successful are the Buell hybrids which are perfect for

43

Photo by Michael A. Riley

The white, pink or blue flowers of Streptocarpus *are often striped on the lower lobes of the corolla. Pictured is one of the 'Olympus' hybrids.*

windowsill, artificial light culture and the greenhouse. These hybrids are more compact in habit with much larger flowers and a fantasy of colors and patterning. The advent of fluorescent light gardening has called for the miniaturization of everything and sinningias are no exception. *Sinningia pusilla* is of mature flowering size in a one-inch pot.

Many hybridizers, such as Martin Mines and Ted Bona, have developed hundreds of new *Sinningia* hybrids which grow to blooming size in a two-and-a-half-inch pot and in every color imaginable, including yellow. All sinningias develop tubers underground and therefore have a definite cycle of growth and dormancy. Some tubers resprout immediately while others remain dormant for a month or two. When growing, they take the same consistent culture as previously discussed. Higher light intensity during the first two weeks as the sprouts emerge from the tubers produces a nice compact crown of leaves prior to bloom.

Many gesneriads are true epiphytes and naturally grow in trees on steep hillsides where they have limited root systems. They often have either a spreading or trailing habit, relatively small leaves and spectacular flowers. All of these qualities make them per-fect candidates for hanging basket culture. Their size can be controlled for culture under lights, but they grow best in a window with higher light intensities. Their habitats in nature are more varied and they can tolerate slightly more erratic watering schedules and temperature fluctuations. Columneas have an enormous range of characteristics and some are true seasonal bloomers while others such as *Columnea* 'Chanticleer' are everblooming. *Nematanthus* have rounded shiny leaves similar to hoya and brightly colored red and orange flowers. Both *Nematanthus* and *Aeschynanthus* prefer higher light intensities and bloom nicely in a south window while columneas, in general, grow best in an east or west exposure. They can be moved outside for the summer as long as they are kept watered.

The diversity within this one plant family is unusual and seemingly infinite. New collections from the Far East and many parts of South America are being introduced. There is *Nautilocalyx* with hairy stems and shiny leaves, *Drymonia* which vines through the trees, *Negria* which are trees on Lord Howe Island and true alpines such as *Jankaea heldreichii* from Mount Olympus. *Bellonia spinosa* has spines, the green and purple spotted flowers of *Capanea grandiflora* are pollinated by bats and the entire genus of *Codonanthe* has a symbiotic relationship with ants. Many other gesneriads are pollinated by hummingbirds and bees. These plants have strikingly colorful flowers and add diversity and interest to an indoor collection.

Saintpaulia 'Pixie Blue' is a miniature with a trailing habit that was bred by Lyndon Lyon. This plant is in a three-inch plastic pot.

Sinningia 'Bright Eyes' is a miniature plant (see pencil point) which thrives in terrariums and under fluorescent lights.

Hoya obscura *has unusual flowers. The plant is
small to medium sized.*

Hoya

Christine M. Burton

H oya is a varied genus. Of the approximate 150 known species, some are succulent but most are not. Some have huge leaves two feet long by four to six inches wide; others have small leaves (a half inch long by an eighth inch wide) while the balance vary in size between those extremes. Some twine and cling to supports by aerial roots, others cascade from tree trunks or baskets. Some flower repeatedly from the same peduncle, others bloom only once from the same peduncle. Some hoyas have few flowers, others many. There are hoyas with large flowers and those with tiny flowers. Flowers come in white, pink, rose, red, purple, brown and yellow. A few have contrasting crowns, a few have contrasting borders on their corollas.

As there is variety among hoyas, there is variety in the selection of media to grow them. There appears to be no "best" potting medium as growers swear by a variety ranging from garden soil to kitty litter. But all growers agree that the chosen growing medium must contain a great deal of drainage material. A mixture of good potting soil with added perlite and fir bark chips for drainage is suitable. One could also use charcoal, shredded tree fern bark, rocks, or shard. Most hoyas grow

---

Christine M. Burton is a trained musician, whose hobby has always been plants. She is the founder of the Hoya Society and editor of its bulletin, "The Hoyan."

In their native habitats hoyas climb tree trunks. This sturdy hoya is growing along with dendrobium orchids in Southwest Sumatra near Ombilin.

best at temperatures above 45 °F and flower best when the temperature is above 70 °F . Most grow naturally in tropical rain forests in the hottest parts of the world so they tolerate hot weather well. Some of those from higher elevations flower better between 70 °F and 80 °F but the plants do not seem to be harmed even at 120 °F which my central Georgia greenhouse has been known to register.

Many report that hoyas will bloom only in sunlight sufficient to cause yellowing of the leaves. I have not found this to be true. I have grown and flowered *H. carnosa* in dense shade. Others bloom in my greenhouse with shade cloth screening 73% of direct sunlight. One factor that I have found to inhibit bloom is air conditioning. Why a hoya that will bloom in a greenhouse at 72 °F will not bloom indoors with the thermostat set at 72 °F is a mystery. But I suspect it's the lack of humidity. I recommend moving hoyas during bloom season to a screened porch or tree limb. . . unless your home is not air conditioned or you have a greenhouse.

Almost all hoyas require a lot of water during hot weather but less during cooler weather. A good rule is to water thoroughly when the potting medium is dry one to two inches down from the top of the soil. During growing season, a balanced fertilizer such as 20-20-20 (or one with less nitrogen if yours are already growing too large) at one-quarter teaspoon per gallon of water at each watering or a slow release fertilizer scratched into the soil. During the cooler winter months many hoya growers use an 0-10-10 formula once or twice.

The only serious hoya pests are mealybugs.

Mites are also said to be a cause of concern but I have never seen mites do permanent damage to hoyas. To a lesser extent scale is a problem. Hoyas are sensitive to some chemical products. The product I have found safest is insecticidal soap. Others recommend rubbing alcohol, onion juice and garlic.

Sadly, few hoyas are available in retail stores. If one wants to grow species, purchase them from mail order sources. Some sources are listed at the close of this article.

Some Recommended Hoyas

Hoya angustifolia is a plant with variable sized fuzzy leaves on thin stalks. In nature it creeps or twines on branches and tree trunks so is adaptable to hanging basket culture. The one-inch clusters of tiny yellowish-pink flowers are borne on long, thin peduncles. It flowers from a few months to a year after planting and after first flowering is quite reliable. Although usually thought of as a miniature in cultivation, in nature it gets quite large.

Hoya australis is available in many forms but most are very slow to bloom and often buds fall without opening. One form exists that has few faults. This one comes from the Solomon Islands. It is often found in commerce under the erroneous labels of *H. bandaensis* and *H. obtusifolia* (both names belong to very different hoyas which are not available). Leaves are round to oblong and bright green with no speckling. Flowers are white, both corolla and corona, with five dots of red showing on the corolla at the base of the crown.

Hoya bella is known as "The Miniature Hoya." The leaves are miniature when compared to those of *H. carnosa* but are far from the smallest hoya leaves. The flowers are medium sized among a genus whose flowers range from a few centimeters in diameter to well over three inches. The plant itself is something else. I have seen three six-inch cuttings grow to fill an 18″ pot with branches cascading over five feet in three years. That is not a miniature. The secret of keeping *H. bella* healthy appears to be to break all the rules by keeping its "feet" wet. Never let it dry out. There are at least three forms of this species, including one with variegated leaves. The easiest to grow appears to be the variety

Paxtonii, (listed by some dealers as sp. #444). It has much larger undulate leaves. Very similar is *H. lanceolata* (also sold by some as *H. sikkimensis*). By far the most beautiful is *H. bella variegata*.

H. carnosa is usually available as "Grandmother's Old Fashioned Wax Plant." Retailers do not tend to sell it, assuming that everyone who wants one has one. The glossy leaves are elliptic in shape and speckled with silver. The pink velvet flowers appear in large clusters. *H. carnosa* may take five or more more years to initiate bloom. The similar *H. motoskei* has lighter flesh colored flowers and round leaves. It is not quite as handsome as *H. carnosa*, due to duller leaves. However, it blooms at a younger age. I would not recommend these two unless one is a collector. Contrary to past thought, *H. motoskei* is not the same species as *H. carnosa*.

Hoya cinnamomifolia has fairly large dull green leaves with lighter colored veins, arising at the leaf base and running parallel to the midrib. The greenish-yellow flowers with blood red crowns appear in large clusters. It is easy to grow. A similar species, only recently in cultivation, is *H. purpureo-fusca*, which has leaves with the same venation. Flowers of *H. purpureo-fusca* differ from those of *H. cinnamomifolia*—they are pubescent and the corolla is purplish brown with purple crowns.

Hoya incrassata is good for a beginning houseplant enthusiast because it is a fast grower. It makes a handsome basket plant very quickly although the flowers are not as conspicuous as most—yellow with a red or rust margin. The margin is visible for only a short time before the flowers reflex and the edges turn under. While the margins are visible it is very beautiful. It blooms freely and repeatedly on the same peduncles throughout the summer months.

Hoya imperialis is a plant for people who have lots of space. It has large leaves, extremely thick stalks and large flowers. The flower clusters usually measure around nine inches in diameter, with individual flowers up to three inches in diameter. Flowers are brownish red with a cream corona. The variety *rauschii,* which is more common in the U.S., has pink blooms.

Invest in the Best and the Brightest

Hibiscus *hybrids are available in many bright colors. Flowers contrast nicely with dark green glossy foliage.*

Sinningia speciosa *was originally collected by Guest Editor, Charles Marden Fitch, in Brazil.*

Top: Hoya bella *is a vine that bears waxy flowers in umbels. The perfection of the individual flowers gives them the appearance of unreality.*

Bottom: *Carts equipped with fluorescent lights can be placed almost anywhere. This one is in the basement. Here is a varied collection of begonias, African violets, and orchids.*

Top: *Miniature rose 'Little Liza' provides a complement and accent for the tea table.*

Bottom: Kalanchoe *'Cinnabar' is a bright splash of color in any surroundings.*

Aechmea fulgens *var.* discolor albo-marginata *displays colorful fruits for a long time.*

Hoya acuta, *left, is trained on a wire loop.*

A collection of haworthias planted in a low dish is a study in shapes, textures and shades of color.

A tiny creeping relative of hoyas Dischidia nummularia *(see pen point at the right for size reference). This epiphytic vine will thrive planted in rough sphagnum moss or a coarse fir bark mix.*

Hoya carnosa *'Exotica' is a variegated cultivar of the easy to grow fragrant-flowered species.*

H. kerrii is the species called "Valentine" or "Sweetheart," formerly called by some U.S. dealers *H. obovata,* a name belonging to another species. The leaves are dull green, notched at the outer end, and pointed at the base. The overall leaf shape is that of a valentine. There are three forms of *H. kerrii* in U.S. trade. One has glabrous leaves; one has pubescent leaves and the third has more or less parchment-like leaves with a little speckling on the upper surface. The similar *H. obovata* has roundish, unnotched leaves and larger flowers, which have a differently shaped corona. It is a much easier plant to grow but lacks the interesting heart-shaped leaves of *H. kerrii.*

Hoya lacunosa is a true miniature having leaves about an inch long by a half-inch wide. Flowers are white with yellow crowns. They are fuzzy little stars tightly curled appearing to be little balls. They have a very clean, pleasant scent. In nature, *H. lacunosa* climbs along tree trunks, where ants build tunnels and nests among its roots and stems. In cultivation this species adapts to growing in a basket.

Hoya macgillivrayii is probably the most beautiful of hoyas. The large thick leaves grow on thin wiry stems that appear too fragile to hold them. The flowers vary in size from clone to clone, from two-and-one-half to three-and-one-quarter inches in diameter, with five to thirteen flowers in each umbel. Color varies from white to deep maroon, depending on light, nutrition or temperature—no one knows just what causes the varying shades, often on the same plant at the same time. There are at least three forms of this hoya available, plus two forms of a closely related one (which may prove to be a variety of it), *H. archboldiana.* The smaller flowered one is the better bloomer. The scent is divine. The only fault in this species is the extremely wide spaced leaves. This spacing means that the plant must be very mature before the plant matches the flowers in beauty, even though the leaves are among the most beautiful of all hoya leaves.

Hoya obscura is a small to medium-sized plant which grows best in a basket. The rather stiff stalks are not as inclined to twine as most hoyas. The leaves are light green with lighter pinnate veining. The leaves of some clones turn quite red in the winter sun. The small flowers are similar to those of *H. lacunosa.* A pink flowered form and a white flowered form are known. *H. obscura* is relatively new to the trade so the price will be rather high. I list it here because so many Hoya Society members have stated it is their favorite. It is very easy to grow and with such popularity should become reasonably priced very soon.

Hoya 'Pink Silver' is a beautiful and easily grown clone of an unknown species. It is almost universally mislabeled *H. purpureo-fusca* by dealers and writers alike. *H. purpureo-fusca* is a different species, currently listed by only one U.S. grower at a ridiculously high price, which will be much lower as more stock is available. 'Pink Silver' is also available as *USDA #353450,* 'Silver Leaf.' The leaves resemble those of *H. carnosa* but often have more silver speckling. Flowers differ principally in being deep maroon with a white crown. The crown is larger and somewhat different in shape. *H.* 'Pink Silver' blooms at a younger age than *H. carnosa* and is much showier. A form from the Philippines has deep red stems and veins (on the underside) and much more silver flecking. The flowers are almost black and the crown even darker. A similar cultivar, 'Red Button,' is popular but not nearly as handsome.

Sold as *H. pubera* or sp. *geri* is a tiny little woody-stemmed hoya with tiny umbels of pinkish flowers. It blooms in the fall with umbels at every node (when young) and over a long period. It is just about everyone's favorite, as it is a miniature well-suited to the light garden.

Hoya shepherdii is the "String Bean Hoya," which, even now is being sold by some as *H. longifolia* (while *H. longifolia* is being sold as something else). *Hoya shepherdii* is easy to grow, blooms when young and can be counted on to bloom each spring. It is interesting for its long skinny leaves, a contrast to the usual ovate or elliptic shaped leaves. *H. shepherdii* is very common, so the price is usually very reasonable.

Hoya serpens is easy to grow but difficult to flower, but all who see a photograph of it want it. The leaves are about the size and shape of a dime, dark green and sparsely hairy. The flowers, which are larger than the leaves, open green, become white and turn pink as they mature. Often all three colors can be seen on a mature plant at the same time. In the past this was erroneously listed as *H. engleriana, H. minima, H. nummularia* (all three different species) and *H. miniata*. This hoya is not recommended for the beginner— excellent in a light garden as it is a true miniature.

Hoyas easy to find in shops, grocers and discount stores are cultivars known as "Indian Ropes," plain and variegated, 'Krimson Queen,' 'Krimson Princess,' and others. These plants are best sought locally. The easiest and most rewarding Indian Rope is one called 'Krinkle 8.' The leaves and stalks, which cascade, are extremely thick. The plant, a vigorous grower, flowers soon and often. Despite the thickness of the stalk, the cascading habit makes for a very graceful appearance in a hanging basket or in a pot on a pedestal. A variegated form of 'Krinkle 8' is available but is not a vigorous grower.

A closely related genus, *Centrostemma,*

has several species worth growing along with hoyas. *Centrostemma multiflora* is available from most hoya dealers, often under the label *Hoya multiflora.*

There are many more hoyas available and more being introduced each season. If you are undecided, most growers will help you select a few to start you off. Also the Hoya Society International sponsors a number of round robins. These help the beginner to learn what others grow and how they grow them. Members often trade plants and cuttings along with knowledge. Recommended dealers:

ad Astra Flora, Route 1, Box 333-A-2, Monticello, GA 31064

Hill 'n Dale, 6427 N. Fruit Avenue, Fresno, CA 93711

Rainforest, 1550 Rycroft Street, Honolulu, HI 96814

Ralph Reardon, 110 Demandre Street, Belle Chasse, LA 70037

For information about The Hoya Society International write to: Christine M. Burton, P.O. Box 54171, Atlanta, GA 30308. 🌿

Hoya 'Hindu Rope' has twisted waxy succulent foliage with varied patterns of cream and green often flushed with pink when grown in bright light.

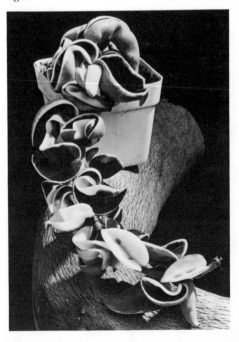

Araucaria heterophylla, *Norfolk Island Pine, is contrasted here with* Dracaena deremensis.

Rheo spathacea, *Moses-in-the-boat, grows on rotting leaves which gather among the coral stones in Mexico.*

Foliage Favorites
for Indoor Gardens

A photo essay by Charles Marden Fitch

Foliage plants are the most adaptable of indoor plants because they need less light than the specimens we grow for flowers. Perhaps the most common foliage plant in offices is the heart-leaf *Philodendron oxycardium,* a species from the jungles of Central America. This philodendron, like its common companions the Chinese Evergreen (*Aglaonema*) is an aroid, a group of lovely plants so suited to indoor gardening that this book gives them a separate family feature. In addition to the many aroids appreciated for

their foliage are species from several genera, all worth considering as indoor decoration. These photographs illustrate some of the choices you will find at well stocked nurseries and mail order gardening firms. 🌿

Foliage plants thrive in a bright window in Spain. Shown are Asparagus densiflorus, *spider plant and variegated ivy.*

Hedera helix *'Itsy-Bitsy' is a miniature ivy. This one is growing in a hanging container.*

Hedera helix *var.* conglomerata *has an upright rather than weeping habit. Planted in a glazed bonsai tray with weathered driftwood and mulched with sphagnum moss, this combination makes a striking centerpiece.*

Helxine soleirolii aurea *has light golden yellow foliage which makes it an attractive ground cover in terrariums or around the base of potted plants.*

Left: Ficus diversifolia *is called mistletoe fig because of the yellow fruits borne on mature specimens.*
Above: *Unusual foliage of some tropical plants:*

Top left: Ficus pumila minima *and* F.p. *var.* quercifolia *(oakleaf); bottom left:* Anthurium polyschistum; *Top right: trailing* Gibasis geniculata *(which will have tiny white flowers).*

Scented Geraniums

Scented-leaf geraniums (Pelargonium).
*This photogram shows the leaves of several
scented geraniums at actual size. Included are* P.
filicifolium *'Fern Leaf' (bottom right),* P. *'Joy
Lucille Variegated' (top left),* P. denticulatum

'Pine' (bottom left), P. graveolens *'Rober's Lemon
Rose' (top right), and* P. x *'Blandfordianum,' a
hybrid of* P. graveolens *and* P. echinatum *(right
center).*

Joy Logee Martin

Interest in scented geraniums has waxed and waned through the years. These plants are native to South Africa and were first introduced into England in 1632. By the end of the 17th century many varieties had been collected. The most useful and popular are the rose scented kinds, *P. capitatum* and *P. graveolens* and their hybrids. Acres of rose scented geraniums were grown in France and Turkey to produce the less expensive rose oil or attar of roses to replace the true oil of roses. It is the fragrance released by the oil glands on the leaves when they are slightly bruised that gives the scented geraniums their charm.

In addition to the rose varieties there are many other scents and flavors; lemon, lime, nutmeg, orange, pineapple, strawberry, coconut, peppermint, pine, etc. Pelargoniums are often classified in catagories such as rose, lemon, fruit scented, mint scented, spice scented. Today some collectors list over 100 varieties. Many are very much alike in form and fragrance, but to the eager collector they all have a place.

A scented geranium revival began in this country in the 1930's when one collector assembled and identified over eighty varieties. Not only is it fun to grow species such as *P. odoratissimum* (apple scented) and *P. parviflorum* from seed, but a sharp eye will often observe different growth, which is how many variegated forms have been discovered, including the lovely *P.* x *fragrans* (nutmeg).

Scented geraniums are easy to grow. Sun loving, they will grow in relatively cool locations as indoor plants. When planted in the garden varieties such as peppermint, *P. tomentosum* will grow to enormous size in one season. The soil should be well-drained, a mixture of equal parts of soil, sand and compost with the addition of a two-and-one-half-inch pot each of lime and bone meal per bushel of soil mix. Take cuttings at any time from tip growth; select half-hardened stems about two-and-one-half inches to three inches long. Dip in rooting powder and place in sand—they will root in about ten days. Or cuttings can be placed in a medium of sand, perlite and peat moss. Temperature for rooting should be 60° to 70° degrees.

Scented geraniums have relatively small flowers of lavender to white. A few exceptions are 'Clorinda' with large rose colored blooms, 'Mrs. Taylor' with smaller umbels of scarlet flowers, 'Pretty Polly' with light pink blooms and 'Apricot' with salmon flowers.

Scented geraniums make excellent standards. If large standards are desired, 'Rose,' 'Clorinda,' 'Pretty Polly,' 'Mrs. Taylor,' and 'Mabel Grey' can be used. For short dwarf standards, 'Little Gem,' 'Lime,' 'Ginger,' 'Lemon Crispum,' 'Prince Rupert Variegated,' and 'Spring Park' are excellent candidates. Choose a plant with a central straight stem and stake it. When the plant has reached a height of about 10 or 12 inches remove the lower leaves and side shoots, leaving about four breaks from the top. When the plant has reached the preferred heights pinch out the center. As it grows pinch out the tip ends to make a round bushy top growth. The plant must be pruned judiciously every three months.

Following is a list of the most fragrant and best growers:

P. graveolens—rose scented

P. graveolens 'Variegatum'—rose scented with pink, white and green leaves

P. crispum 'Lemon Crispum'—the finger-bowl geranium

P. crispum 'Prince Rupert'—a fine variegated lemon scented

P. 'Mabel Grey'—lemon verbena fragrance, holds its scent when dried

P. odoratissimum—apple scented

P. x *limoneum*—cinnamon scented

P. x 'Toronto'—ginger scented

P. fragrans 'Logeei'—spice scented

P. nervosum—lime scented

P. x *fragrans* 'Variegatum'—nutmeg scented

P. citriodorum—orange scented

P. 'Spring Park'—lemon-strawberry scented

P. tomentosum—peppermint scented

P. x 'Clorinda'—pungent, eucalyptus scent

P. quercifolium 'Fair Ellen'—oak leaf, pungent scent

Joy Logee Martin is director of Logee's Greenhouses in Danielson, CT, and writes, lectures, and teaches about horticulture, especially herbs and begonias. Her collection includes more than 75 varieties of scented geraniums. Mrs. Martin is well known for her articles in popular gardening magazines, and as a flower show judge.

*Why not enjoy
America's number one flower
through the seasons . . .*

Miniature Roses Under Fluorescent Lights

Charles Marden Fitch

You can have fragrant roses all year round by growing miniatures under fluorescent lights. For gardeners in cold temperature climates it is especially thrilling to pick roses during the winter. Rose experts also like to grow miniatures under lights so they can have top quality blooms for rose shows. I like growing miniatures under lights because the tiny flowers are so abundant, colorful, often fragrant, and last many days when cut in bud. Best of all, the miniature rose bushes are cold hardy so after enjoying them under lights a season or two, one can plant them in the garden for years of outdoor pleasure. This makes space for new kinds the next winter.

Light and Temperature*

Like the larger roses, miniatures must have intense light to produce the best blooms. With low light they will grow but flowers will be few, colors abnormal, stems weak. My best indoor miniature roses are grown under four 40-watt broad spectrum fluorescent lamps. The bushes under broad spectrum tubes have more flowers, better color and sturdier stems than the same varieties grown under plain household lamps such as cool white or warm white.

Miniature roses produce buds on new growth, so keeping them growing is important. I provide 14 to 16 hours of light per 24-hour period. Seedlings will bloom faster if given up to 18 hours of light. Keep foliage close to the lamps but watch that buds do not touch the tubes. Although tubes are cool compared to incandescent bulbs, they will still burn leaves or buds that push against them.

*Also consult information in the feature "House Plants Under Lights" on page 82 of this issue.

My miniatures thrive under intermediate conditions, with night hours 58 to 62 °F, daytime highs up to 78 °F. If grown cooler, they slow down and flowers last longer; if grown warmer, they tend to have lighter-colored flowers which last fewer days. Since these are cold-hardy plants they can accept very chilly temperatures, but the object of having them indoors is to get flowers on new growth. Therefore nights of 60 to 65 °F, combined with bright 14 to 16 hour days, are the most practical. Keep relative humidity between 50 and 60 percent. Low humidity encourages red spider mites and smaller flowers; too high a humidity, especially with still air, encourages fungus.

Potting

The smallest miniature roses thrive in three to four inch pots. Taller ones grow well in six to ten inch containers. Slightly restrict root room if you wish to keep bushes compact. Plastic pots are excellent, but clay are also suitable if you avoid letting the bushes dry out completely at the roots. Place a half to one inch of gravel in the bottom of the pot, then add a chunk or two of hardwood charcoal, followed by coarse unmilled sphagnum moss, then the potting mixture.

I find commercially prepared potting mixes suitable when the package directions are followed. Some types contain fertilizers,

Miniature rose 'Green Ice' makes a bushy semi-trailing plant which is suitable for hanging baskets. Start the plants under lights and when buds appear, hang in a sunny window or sunporch.

A miniature rose blossom, held between two fingers demonstrates the size of the flower.

These miniature roses thrive under broad spectrum fluorescent lamps where 12 to 16 hours of fluorescent light supplements morning's natural light. Shown left to right are: 'Claret,' 'Linda,' 'Mimi,' 'Green Ice,' 'Littlest Angel,' 'Pearl Dawn,' 'Seabreeze.' The pots sit on moist gravel for added humidity. Two Cryptanthus plants provide contrast.

Plant miniature rose seed in flats filled with milled sphagnum moss mixed with perlite and vermiculite. Dust seeds with Rootone to stimulate roots and prevent fungus problems. Space seeds one to two inches apart so seedlings have room to grow before transplanting.

Perfection is possible even though the size is diminutive—see ring for scale.

others grow nice plants only when fertilizer is provided in solution every few days. The mix should be slightly acid and retain moisture without getting soggy. Miniature roses should never dry out completely at the roots.

Ordering, Selections

Mail-order miniature rose specialists will send you sturdy bushes anytime. For indoor growing start with dormant bushes as sent by many nurseries, or pot active bushes, but let them stay outdoors in the fall to early winter until they experience six to eight weeks of cold weather. As cold-hardy plants, miniature roses should have a dormant period each year to make the best growth and keep a compact shape.

Most suitable for growing under lights are micro miniature hybrids and selections that can be pruned to stay under eight inches tall. With the recent great interest in miniature roses many hybrids have been developed, and each year a batch of new ones is introduced. Some of my favorite proven selections are: 'Cinderella', a compact, very double white blushed pink; 'Littlest Angel', a micro mini with wider than high habit, perfectly formed golden yellow half-inch flowers on a three to four inches tall plant; 'Magic Carrousel', a sturdy fragrant white with red edges, excellent form, long lasting; 'Party Girl', a fragrant apricot yellow of exhibition form, adaptable

habit; 'Pacesetter', a perfect miniature of classic hybrid tea type, white sometimes blushed pink, fragrant; 'Rise 'n' Shine', the best yellow mini for fragrance, form, color; and 'Zinger', with brilliant crimson red flowers which show a contrasting yellow center when mature.

Culture

Miniature roses will produce the first flowers six to eight weeks after starting growth after a dormant period. Once active they continue to produce flowers for many months. Provide a balanced fertilizer in solution every other watering or apply timed release fertilizers designed for roses. Active roses need a steady supply of nutrients and water. You can prune back bushes to keep them compact but always leave at least one third of the growth.

Miniature roses indoors are less likely to get foliage fungus if you keep air circulation constant. I use a fan going all the time in my basement light garden area and also in the greenhouse. Wash bushes with room-temperature water every month to discourage red spider mites. Miniatures can be treated with the same fungicides and pesticides used on outdoor roses.

*Also consult information in the feature "House Plants Under Lights" on page 82 of this issue.

Learning More:

For more details on these tiny plants please see *The Complete Book of Miniature Roses* by Charles Marden Fitch (Hawthorn/Dutton pub.)

Tropical Bulbs For The Home

Don Richardson

The great beauty of tropical bulbs can and should be appreciated in the home. Yet many are purchased, then lost, because their cultural requirements are not well understood. Several factors should be considered when selecting tropical bulbs: size of the mature plant; flowering season; temperature and light requirements.

These factors are important for various reasons. As an example, let us consider the lovely *Agapanthus*. Though not a true bulb, it is often sold in stores with amaryllis *(Hippeastrum)* and other bulbs. The normal flowering season of *Agapanthus* is July and August, hardly a time when most people need or want a three-to-four-foot plant to bloom in the home. Granted, there are several dwarf types, but they would be better used in tubs on the terrace at that season. A better choice would be the amaryllis *(Hippeastrum)* itself, which can be flowered from December to April, a time when indoor growers are more likely to appreciate it.

Bulbous plants usually need a dry resting period which corresponds to the dry season in their native habitat. The majority of flowering bulbs need good light and a well drained, friable potting soil plus some bone meal. Supplemental fluorescent light can easily be provided in the home if light intensity is too low. Bulbs preferring cooler temperatures, such as lachenalias, may be grown in a cool room or on a porch where temperatures will remain above freezing.

Amaryllis

Perhaps the best known, and certainly among the most colorful tropical bulbs are the modern amaryllis *(Hippeastrum)* hybrids with large, broad, open flowers that can measure eight or nine inches across. The bulbs, which are of good size, have two stout flower stalks. Red, scarlet, pink, salmon and orange are some of the colors found in these hybrids, and plants with striped flowers are not uncommon.

Enterprising dealers often sell amaryllis bulbs already potted. If you buy bare bulbs, which are available from November through March, pot them up in a good soil mix, covering about half the bulb with soil and leaving the top part exposed. Slightly tight potting, as in six-inch pots, is best.

Place the potted amaryllis bulbs where they will receive gentle heat from below, and do not water for about two weeks. The flower spike will usually appear first, then the leaves. Give plants more water after leaves start growing. It may be necessary to support the spike, since bulbs often flower before making roots.

Amaryllis bulbs are expensive, so good after-care is advisable. Cut off the flower spike when blooms fade. Keep foliage growing all summer, with plenty of water and food to build up strength for the following year's flowers. The pots can be plunged in the

Top: Dramatic flowers of Dutch type hybrid amaryllis.

Bottom Left: Eucharis grandiflora *has foliage that resembles an* Aspidistra. *Fragrant white flowers are produced two or three times a year if the bulbs are given dry rests between growth periods.*

Bottom Right: Cyclamen persicum *hybrids have flowers in shades of red, purple, pink and white. The mottled foliage is attractive as well.*

Don Richardson was a professional horticulturist at Greentree Estates in Manhasset, N.Y. He was known for his knowledgeable approach to growing orchids and other tropical exotics.

Clivia miniata *is an amaryllis relative. The leaves are wide and leathery and the roots thick and tuberous. The fragrant flowers are orange with creamy yellow centers appearing in the spring. Clivias come from South Africa.*

ground outside for the summer. If you keep them inside, give them good light and water until October, when they can be rested.

In December or January, top dress the pots, scratching away some of the surface soil and replacing old potting mix with some good soil enriched with bone meal. Any small side bulbs can be removed and grown on, or they can be left to form a specimen plant which will have several spikes. The flowers may not be as large as with commercially produced bulbs, but a pot with more flowers is very pleasing, even when individual flowers are smaller. These showy hybrid amaryllis, developed from several South American species, may be listed under confusing names, so selecting them by color is a practical way to order.

Clivia and Lachenalia

The Kaffir-lily or *Clivia* (formerly *Imantophyllum*) is in the same botanical family as the amaryllis. Clivias are from South Africa and are probably better all-round houseplants than amaryllis because they have good foliage through the year. However, we cannot expect the same wide range of color as that obtained from amaryllis. Clivias have fleshy roots, not true bulbs, so pot single crowns in six-inch pots and larger specimens of several crowns in ten- or twelve-inch pots or tubs. There should be no drastic dry rest, just a moderately dry period in December and

January. Clivias are rich feeders so give liquid fertilizers freely during the growing season.

Plants available are usually hybrids of *Clivia miniata* and *C.* x *cyrtanthiflora*. They bloom in winter, bearing clusters of lilylike flowers in shades of orange, red or pink on eighteen-inch stems. Blooms last for two weeks when cut. Clivias resent disturbance, so grow them for several years in the same container before repotting. Division of the plants can be done after flowering. Clivias are able to grow in low light but need good strong light for an abundance of flowers.

The Cape-cowslips *(Lachenalia),* also from South Africa, belong to the Lily Family. They must have a complete dry rest after growth is complete. They prefer cooler temperatures, needing only enough warmth to keep out the frost. A 50 °F night temperature is ideal. The bulbs are small, so a half dozen can be planted in a six-inch pot, with the tips of the bulbs just at the surface. They like good light and if kept cool, can be enjoyed for two months. Strong bulbs will produce three or four spikes of tubular, bell-shaped flowers. Those usually offered are cultivars of *Lachenalia aloides;* 'Aurea' is bright orange-yellow; 'Nelsonii' is bright yellow; 'Quadricolor' is red at the base, greenish-yellow in the middle, and green at the outer edges.

Lachenalias make attractive hanging baskets. If you wish to grow them this way, prepare a wire basket with moss lining. Plant some of the bulbs upside down at the base, about three inches apart, plant others on their sides at the sides of the basket, then plant still others upright at the top, filling in the potting mix as you go. Any *Lachenalia* can be used, but perhaps the best for this purpose would be *L. bulbiferum* which is red-purple and yellow in color. After flowering, watering should continue until the leaves start to yellow. Then dry the plants off until the end of August when the bulbs can be repotted. Small bulbils can be grown on to flower in two years.

Eucharis, Veltheimia, Others

Eucharis, the Amazon-lily, is another bulb related to amaryllis. Flowers are white, large and showy, but the plants are also of substantial size. Native of Colombia, they require temperatures of 65-75 °F and higher in summer. *Eucharis grandiflora,* sometimes listed as *E. amazonica,* is the species usually offered. The stalked, oblong leaves are dark green, bold and attractive. Plants should never be allowed to dry out completely. A short period of drier treatment in autumn is often advocated, but ours are watered and fed the year round and produce two crops of flowers a year. They are four inches across and are borne on scapes about two feet high. Plants in twelve-to-fourteen-inch tubs are very handsome, and the flowers last well when cut.

Veltheimia is a small genus of South African bulbs belonging to the Lily Family. The bulbs are fairly large, and just one in a six-inch pot makes quite a show, although I prefer larger pots with several bulbs. The flowers are borne in dense clusters on a stout spike or raceme. They are pendant and tubular, and in *V. viridifolia* they are reddish with greenish tips. There may be up to thirty flowers a spike, each flower one and one-half inches long. Veltheimias should be dried off when the twelve-inch-long straplike foliage turns yellow. Allow about two months dry rest. Plants prefer cool conditions.

Scilla peruviana, unlike our garden scillas, is not winter hardy in the cooler parts of the United States. Despite its botanical name as well as various misleading common names (Cuban-lily, Peruvian hyacinth), it is from the Mediterranean region. We grow this scilla under the same conditions as *Veltheimia.* The deep green leaves are nine-to-twelve inches long and radiate from the bulb. There are 50 to 100 blue-violet flowers in a dense raceme on a short scape, with the lower flowers opening first. To me, the inflorescence in bud is perfectly beautiful. There is also a white form, *S. peruviana* 'Alba', but the flower heads are usually smaller. Scillas are in the Lily Family.

Cyrtanthus is a genus of plants in the Amaryllis Family. From South and East Africa come up to 40 species, but few are seen in cultivation. Undoubtedly the best for home-growing are the *Cyrtanthus mackenii* hybrids. The bulbs are small so plant five or six in a five-inch pot. Because *C. mackenii* is a swamp plant, hence unaccustomed to a dry period, its progeny can be kept growing most of the year in the home. The narrow leaves are small, and there are five to ten tubular, fragrant flowers, each about two inches long. It is best to repot the bulbs every year since they make many bulbils. Grow them cool.

Vallota speciosa (purpurea), sometimes called Scarborough-lily, comes from South Africa. It is related to *Cyrtanthus* and has been hybridized with it. The plant and flowers are more like amaryllis *(Hippeastrum),* although *Vallota* usually flowers in August. Once potted it is advisable to let the bulbs become crowded in the container.

Repotting of *Vallota* is best done in June, at which time the crowded bulbs can be transferred to a larger container. Give plants a rest in winter, but do not let them become completely dry. Water them freely and feed them well with liquid fertilizer when they are growing. The flowers are bright scarlet, three-to-four inches long, several to a scape.

Cyrtanthus mackenii *hybrid. Flowers of coral peach are borne on slender stems arising from a small bulb.*

HOUSEPLANTS IN APARTMENTS

Elvin McDonald

Apartment gardeners, as compared to those who live in houses, typically have less control over light and temperatures, less space for plants and supplies, and usually no place to grow except indoors. Despite these seeming limitations, it is possible to obtain great satisfaction in all seasons from a vast array of plants cultivated for flowers, foliage and fragrance.

Let's imagine you're in New York and have come to visit my garden, which happens to be entirely indoors in a modern high-rise building. The street below is busy, noisy and polluted, yet as soon as you enter my door, all that seems far away. Throughout the apartment, dozens if not hundreds of plants grow in every room, all in clay pots with matching saucers. Moisture evaporating through the unglazed walls helps maintain humidity at a desirable 35 percent or more even during the winter heating season. Moist earth and clay also smell good.

Our tour begins in the entry area, which accommodates a round dining table. The cloth is floor-length for good reason: concealed underneath in autumn are 30 pots of resting amaryllis that spend spring and summer in windows soaking up the sun's energy and, come winter, give it back in a spectacular flower show.

Next to the table is an old marble-top dresser. Here I display seasonal harvest from my weekend garden in the country. In autumn there'll be a big pumpkin, some winter squash and a basket of Indian corn. A bouquet of fragrant bittersweet berries may

remain until spring. At Christmas this space is occupied by living wreaths of hoya and ivy tied with red plaid bows and a bowl of spicy pomander balls.

*Bookshelf light garden: two 20-watt tubes light tiny trees—*Serissa, Carissa, Leptospermum—*and a "lawn" of clipped baby's-tears* (Soleirolia), *all in Chinese and Japanese pots.*

Nearby in floor-to-ceiling bookshelves that divide the dining and living areas, one shelf 12 by 30 inches is lighted by two 20-watt fluorescent lights that burn 16 hours out of every 24. Here I show off my prettiest miniature plants at any given time: *Begonia prismatocarpa, Gesneria cuneifolia,* teacup *Sinningia* species and hybrids, myrtle trees nine inches tall, insectivorous sundew and venus' flytrap, backed by small-leaved ivies espaliered on eight-inch circles of wire. If

---

Elvin McDonald, gardener/writer, is Director of Special Projects at BBG. His twice-weekly column, "Plants in the Home," is syndicated by King Features.

Photos by Elvin McDonald

Corn plants (Dracaena massangeana) *trained to tree-form standards, frame view from bed-sitting room to living room. Screwpine* (Pandanus) *on pedestal behind piano gives tree impression.*

there aren't any flowers, I may add cut blooms, maybe wax begonias from window plants, freesias from the florist, or short sprays of red crab apples.

As we enter the living room, notice there are seasonal flowering plants sitting in baskets on the floor. In autumn, chrysanthemums and Jerusalem cherries; at Christmas poinsettias and narcissus; toward spring, cyclamen, azalea, cineraria and calceolaria. Under the table lamps are low-light vines such as silver pothos, trained into tidy mounds.

Columneas tend to be too trailing in habit to accommodate under lights. However, training on an eight-inch circle of wire solves the problem and seems to encourage bloom.

The windows all along one wall face south but receive direct sun only about half the time, owing to a tall building across the street. A giant bird of paradise (*Strelitzia nicolai*) reaches nearly wall to wall, floor to ceiling but no, it doesn't bloom—not enough sun, heat and humidity. Foliage plants surround the furniture, some sitting on the floor in pebble humidity trays, others boosted on pedestals or cascading from hanging baskets. These include ferns, philodendrons, screw-pine *(Pandanus)*, Norfolk Island pine and evergreen amaryllids—*Clivia, Eucharis* and *Vallota*—that flower in season.

A row of tall sansevierias thrives in low light and divides the living room proper from a bed sitting room, entered through an archway formed by two eight-foot pleomeles. Dracaenas—*fragrans,* 'Janet Craig,' *massangeana, deremensis* 'Warneckii'—literally cover the walls of these rooms. Bromeliads grow from bark mounts and wall pots hang from structural pillars that extend at right angles into the brightest window light.

Now we head toward the bedrooms, via a hallway that was originally dark and useless. By adding fluorescent-lighted shelves floor to ceiling at either end, I gained 24 square feet of growing space and one of the most appealing areas of the apartment. It is these gardens that offer me a place to potter and putter in the middle of the night. Temperatures on the bottom shelves are often 10 degrees cooler than the top ones—and allow me to succeed with a refreshing variety of plants in only a few square feet of floor space.

In the first and smaller of the two bedrooms I have low-light foliage plants closest to the door, farthest from the windows: *Aspidistra, Dracaena,* miniature *Spathiphyllum clevelandii,* which is rarely without its white peace-lily spathes, beautiful-leaved calatheas and a big basket of *Amomum cardamom,* whose leaves give off a wonderful aroma when stroked.

In the sunny windows I have orchids (*Cattleya, Laelia,* equitant *Oncidium, Dendrobium, Brassavola*), Chinese hibiscus, big snowflake trevesias, which belong to the aralia family, a braided-trunk coffee tree grown from seeds, a *Schefflera arboricola* trained into a tree, and a weeping *Ficus benjamina* that spreads its branches protectively over the bed. Rabbit's-foot ferns and trailing African violets grow in wall pots, again attached to structural pillars at right angles to the windows.

The other bedroom measures about 15 by 18 feet and also has windows across one wall.

Two 30-watt fluorescent tubes over each shelf give 12 square feet of ideal growing space in what was previously a dark, useless interior hallway. Plants on top shelf can be 10 degrees warmer than those on the bottom.

It took me several years to fully understand how I could use this space to best advantage for gardening. Because the apartment is surrounded by other heated spaces, I rarely use the heating unit which is located directly under the windows. I also prefer to keep a window open slightly at night. The result is that plants growing next to the glass experience a cool environment in winter— mid 50's at night, up to 70 °F on a sunny day. This suits geraniums (the Deacon hybrids are recommended for winter bloom; I also have many different scented types), rosemary, bay and parsley. The cool nights bring flowers on holiday cactus (even without long nights and short days) and keep sweet-olive scenting the air September to May.

Plants a few feet back from the windows are slightly warmer and include a variety of begonias, tropical lindens, *Crinum* or milk-and-wine lily, 'Maid of Orleans' jasmine, a bonsai *Schefflera arboricola* and flowering maple. A walk-in closet in the interior is outfitted with a three-shelf fluorescent-light garden measuring two by four feet and provides a perfect place for tropicals—mottle-leaf *Paphiopedilum* and *Phalaenopsis* orchids, African violets, episcias, everblooming *Evolvulus glomeratus* (a bushy morning-glory relative having one-inch heavenly blue flowers), and a collection of small-leaved culinary basils. In late winter and spring this closet light garden serves as a factory for sprouting seeds and rooting cuttings destined for my garden in the country.

The kitchen, at the opposite end of the apartment, is my potting shed. Soil mixes are kept in plastic dishpans on top of the cabinets. Empty pots are stored clean on open shelving, along with vases and baskets. I believe a wellness approach to health is best for plants, as for people. Stay in touch, keep the leaves squeaky clean with mild soap and water and few bugs will bother. For the occasional and inevitable infestations of brown scale, mealybugs, white fly and spider-mite I use nothing stronger than sprays of rubbing alcohol or an insecticidal soap such as Safer's.

Success with an apartment garden depends on the same practices as in a house or outdoors. Plan ahead for when you want color. Determine a planting schedule. I make notes in my datebook and try to keep planting

Outdoor garden art forms such as topiary and espalier can be practiced indoors, using home-made or purchased wire or wood forms.

appointments the same as I do social and business commitments.

Take advantage of microclimates that exist in every growing area—find the cold and hot spots. If too much or too little heat is a problem, a small circulating fan may be the answer. I use both a fan and a cool-vapor humidifier in my closet light garden.

Too much light is rare but if there isn't enough, add some fluorescents, perhaps in a utilitarian space. You'll get the benefits of having a place where plants can be grown well, and can then bring them on occasion to enjoy and share where you and your family live and entertain. If available space for lights is chilly, enclose this garden in plastic; heat from the fixtures makes quite a difference and evaporating moisture boosts humidity to nurture growth.

Fragrance is important to me, and not just because I live in an asphalt jungle. Sweet-olive (*Osmanthus fragrans*), 'Maid of Orleans' jasmine, and citrus gardenia (*Mitriostigma axillare*) are rarely without flowers. From Thanksgiving to Valentine's Day I force pots of tender narcissus (paper-whites, 'Soleil d'Or' and Chinese sacred lily), Dutch hyacinths and lily-of-the-valley. There are also bowls and shallow baskets of potpourri dispersed about the apartment, annually replenished with sweet petals and pungent leaves picked from my country garden.

Another premise I work from is that an apartment garden needs a basic framework provided by evergreen foliage plants. Into this can be set seasonal flowering plants, bouquets of cut or dried flowers and stylish or whimsical topiaries. In spring and summer when I am preoccupied with my country garden, the basic foliage of my apartment garden needs little care.

One needn't have both an indoor and an outdoor garden, but it definitely helps—both gardens and the gardener. The stakes I use indoors, to hold top-heavy amaryllis flowers as well as frames for espaliers and vines, are frugally pruned from shrubbery borders outdoors. A dollar saved on supplies is a dollar to spend on plant materials. Every pot indoors is mulched so that no bare soil shows, also to save moisture and give off earthy smells: pine needles, sheet moss collected from the woods, pebbles from a creek bed.

Indoor gardens, like those outdoors, always need something done, but inside there is a distinct advantage: most of the work, which I know is among the most effective therapies in the world, can be done night or day, wet or dry weather. Training coleus trees, ivy wreaths and creeping ficus topiaries has helped me stop smoking. Planting tiny begonia seeds and finding green babies can bring light into the darkest night. Reach for a plant instead of a pill, a drink or a cigarette, and I promise, you will not be disappointed. ❦

Giant bird of paradise dominates sunny window in living room, with lemon geranium espalier, rosemary wreath, Deacon geraniums for winter bloom and peace lily for flowers all year.

Growing Houseplants From Seed

Steven A. Frowine

Growing plants from seed to maturity is the ultimate achievement for any gardener. Although most gardeners buy their houseplants as mature or small plants, some houseplants, especially some of the bright-blooming pot plants, are very easily grown from seed. Later in this article I will give you specific cultural pointers for some of these plants, but first let's discuss general seed sowing principles.

The Basics

Be sure to obtain fresh seed. The seed packets will have stamped on the back the year of intended use. Older seed will have a lower germination rate. If you obtain seeds from friends, be sure they have been harvested and stored properly. If seeds are not mature, or if they have been incorrectly stored, germination will be poor to nonexistent.

Look on the seed packet or refer to a gardening book to determine how long it takes for the particular plant you are growing to mature from seed to flower. This will give you some idea of the best time for sowing. This information is extremely helpful if you would like to grow gloxinias, calceolarias or other pot plants for gift giving at Christmas or Mother's Day.

By altering the temperature and light intensity, it is possible to somewhat regulate the speed of the growth of these pot plants. If the plants are growing too slowly, increase the amount of light by putting them in a brighter window or extending the number of hours you burn the fluorescent tubes and increase the temperatue by 5 to 10 °F; to slow down growth, reduce the temperature by 5 to 10 °F.

Houseplant seeds are valuable and, many times, very small. To protect your investment, it's usually best to use a commercial seed starting formula available through mail order suppliers or at any garden center. These potting materials are lightweight, easy to handle and to obtain and are sterile so you will not be bothered with weed seeds, or insect and disease problems. If you don't have access to one of these soilless mixes, you can make your own by blending together two parts of sphagnum peat moss, one part perlite and one part vermiculite. This mix, as well as the commercial ones, can be used to start virtually all houseplants from African violets to succulents, including cacti.

Seedlings Require Tender Loving Care

For best germination, seeds require high soil moisture and humidity and warm soil temperatures; most seeds will germinate at around 70 °F. If the soil temperature is below 70 °F, especially if the plants are tropical, you will notice a much reduced germination rate and it will take longer for the seeds to sprout. Low soil temperatures can be caused by moisture evaporating from the seed containers (if they are not covered with plastic or glass), by watering the seedling tray with cold tap water, or by locating the seedling container close to a draft. There are simple steps you can take to ensure high soil temperatures: use a heating cable or propagation mat with a thermostat; place the seed container on top

Steven A. Frowine is Staff Horticulturist and Manager of Public Relations at the W. Atlee Burpee Company. He is an avid indoor and outdoor gardener who has a special love for orchids. Mr. Frowine has gardened in Hawaii, Ohio, Missouri, and Pennsylvania.

Exacum affine *'Tiddly Winks' grows easily from seed and provides a bright splash of color.*

of fluorescent light fixture (the ballast gives off heat) or on top of a refrigerator where the condenser provides bottom heat.

Providing adequate light for seedlings is critical; once they are spindly from lack of light, they never seem to recover. A bright window or greenhouse will sometimes supply enough light, but fluorescent lights are more dependable. They are an ideal light source for germinating and growing seedlings because their light intensity is strong without the accompanying heat found with direct sunlight. Also, with fluorescent lights you can control the amount of light by moving the plants closer or further away from the tubes, or by increasing or decreasing the number of hours per day the tubes burn.

Most seedlings will germinate and grow

Herbs have always been popular as winter houseplants. Pictured here is sweet basil, left and 'Green Bouquet.'

under a two-tube or four-tube fluorescent fixture. Use cool-white or a 50/50 blend of cool-white and warm-white tubes. Burn the lights for 12 to 16 hours. To accelerate growth burn the tubes for longer, up to 24 hours a day. Most seedlings will grow stockiest when the tips of their leaves are placed just a few inches from the tubes. The exceptions are shade-loving houseplants like African violets and foliage plants; they can be grown 6-12″ from the lights.

Seed Sowing Techniques

First gather all the materials you will need—seeds, sterile potting material, containers, and pots. Small, four to six inch pots are usually ideal; in this size pot you can sow the seeds far enough apart so they can grow large before they must be transplanted. It is best to sow separate varieties or types of plants in each pot because various plants have different germination requirements and don't sprout at the same time. Other items you will need include labels (use plastic ones; they don't rot), a clear plastic bag or sheet of glass and a pencil or permanent marker (not a ball-point pen; they are not waterproof!).

It is important that the containers used for sowing seeds be sterile. If they are not new pots, they should be scrubbed thoroughly and then soaked overnight in a solution of one part liquid chlorine bleach to nine parts water. This will remove algae and kill disease organisms. Fill the containers with damp potting material. Using a flat object like a piece of wood or bottom of a clean pot, firm the soil in the pot so it is level. Tamp the potting soil to about one half inch below the pot's rim. Don't use drainage or crock material in the bottom of the pots. It is usually dirty, can harbour disease organisms, and with well-drained commercial potting mixes, it is unnecessary.

Sowing larger seeds like geranium is pretty simple. Each seed can be placed about one-quarter inch apart on top of the soil mix. Cover seeds with a layer of potting soil or milled sphagnum moss to a depth of about two-and-one-half times the diameter of the seed.

If the seed to be sown is dust-fine like wax begonias and gesneriads, it's a good idea, before the seed is sown, to sift a one-quarter inch layer of milled sphagnum moss on top of the potting soil. This seeding "bed" will prevent the seed from falling into soil crevices which would bury it too deep and prevent it from sprouting.

Sowing these tiny seeds can be difficult. To make it easier, blend them with a teaspoon or so of very fine sand or sugar, put this mixture in a salt shaker, and sprinkle it on the surface of the seeding bed. The sugar or sand dilutes the seed and makes it easier to spread it out. I usually forsake this sugar or salt method and merely take a pinch of this fine seed and carefully rub the seeds between my fingers. I watch where they hit on the sphagnum moss layer and try to sow them as evenly and thinly as possible. Since these seeds are so small, it is best not to cover them.

Next place the pots of sown seed in a container of warm water (100-120 °F). This will penetrate the potting material faster than cold water and will cause the seeds to sprout quicker. The water level in the container of water should come only to the pot's rim. Leave the pots in the water a few hours, until the soil is thoroughly wet. If the surface of soilless material or milled sphagnum moss resists wetting, mist lightly with warm water until it is damp. Next, cover the pot with a pane of glass, or slip it into a clear plastic bag (plastic is safer). Place the covered container in a bright, warm place that does not receive direct sunlight.

Most houseplant seeds will sprout in seven to ten days. After they sprout, open the plastic bag or slide the glass pane to expose half of the container. This will help the seedlings gradually adjust to their new environment. Put the seedlings in a bright window or place them four to six inches from fluorescent lights.

After the seedlings have two sets of true leaves (these are much larger than the first "seed leaves" or cotyledons), they can be transplanted. If there is enough space in the original container, allow them to grow until they begin to crowd each other. When transplanting houseplant seedlings, don't put them in too large a pot. In most cases you will want to put them into a two to three inch pot. If they are larger growing plants, they could be moved up later to a six inch pot.

Houseplants to Try From Seed

Herbs have always been popular as winter houseplants. Some of them are easy to grow, compact, and are handy for adding a special touch to a winter salad or soup. Herbs that are recommended for growing indoors are the small-growing basils such as Green Bouquet Basil, parsley, both the Italian and extra curled dwarf, and chives. Herbs grow best in a sunny window or under fluorescent lights in a cool, 55-65°, area.

Some pot plants are ideally suited for a cool greenhouse, a bright window or a cool spot in the basement under fluorescent lights. Special compact varieties of cinerarias, salpiglossis, snapdragons, calceolarias and primroses are perfect for providing dazzling color during the winter.

Annuals should be grown more often as indoor pot plants. They are brightly colored and easy to grow. Good choices include the dwarf varieties of exacum, coleus, celosia, Pot n' Patio asters, and French marigolds such as Happy Days, Cheerful, Queen Sophia, Pigmy, Pretty Joy and Naughty Marietta. These marigolds will bloom in four to five inch pots. To make the plants more bushy, pinch them

when they have about three to four sets of leaves. Sow in early October for bloom in mid-to-late January, late November for early to mid-March bloom, and March for May to June flowering. Impatiens are also an ideal pot plant. Choose those varieties which are very compact like the Accent series. When you sow the seed, be sure not to cover them; they sprout best when the seeds are exposed to light.

Fibrous or wax begonias are also candidates for indoor growing from seed. Even though the minuscule size of the seed is discouraging, they are easy to grow once they sprout. Try the small-growing varieties such as the Cocktail Series or Linda, Scarletta, or Thousand Wonders Red or White. Calico is another attractive begonia with bronze and green foliage.

One of the favorite annuals that you can grow from seed is the geranium (*Pelargonium*). Newer hybrids are vigorous and bloom in 15 to 17 weeks. Try Showgirl, Sprinter Series, Rose Diamond, Cherry Border and Earliana.

Many tropical flowering plants are also easy to grow from seed. Most of the gesneriads like gloxinias, kohlerias, smithianthas and African violets are perfectly suited for light gardening. All of them do have small seed, but once they start growing they are not difficult. Gloxinias (or more correctly sinningias) are one of my favorite plants to grow from seeds for holiday gift giving. I start them four to six months before they are needed. Gloxinias respond to increased light so if you want to accelerate growth put the plants in a brighter spot or burn your fluorescent tubes longer. New streptocarpus hybrids from seed are also appearing on the market. These hybrids are beautiful additions to any indoor garden.

A couple of other delightful and unusual houseplants to grow from seed are the dwarf crape myrtle (Little Chief is a good variety) and the dwarf pomegranate. Since both of these are not commonly seen grown as miniature pot plants, they attract attention from fellow gardeners looking for something new.

Growing houseplants from seed is fun and easy. And one of the best reasons I know for growing houseplants from seed is that you will always have extra plants you can share with your gardening friends!

Containers and Potting Mixes

Elvin McDonald

The pot and what we fill it with play major supporting roles to that of the star in this production, the plant. Success is possible in everything from the ridiculous to the sublime, from an old shoe to a Ming dynasty bonsai pot, which in turn might be filled with anything from a single raw ingredient, garden soil, to a complexity of pasteurized ingredients measured according to recipe and mixed under sterile conditions.

Selecting the right pot

Most pots are clay or plastic. Clay weighs more, an advantage if you need to anchor a top-heavy plant, a disadvantage when paying freight or lifting, unless you can turn pot moving into productive exercise. Plants growing in clay require more water than those in plastic, since moisture transpires through the porous, unglazed walls. This can be an advantage for air and desert plants, and can have a welcome cooling effect for pots outdoors in summer.

Both clay and plastic pots are subject to cracking if frozen while filled with soil. However, if idled pots are emptied, cleaned, sorted and stacked, then stored where they will be frozen through winter, this can be a painless way to disinfect.

Plastic pots are indisputably easier to clean than clay. Minor encrustations of mineral salts, found mostly at the rim and around drainage holes, rub or brush off readily after soaking overnight in water that was hot at the beginning. Mineral salts cling much more tenaciously to clay, but can be softened by adding one-half cup vinegar to each gallon of soaking water. Besides a stiff brush and soap pads, you may need a knife to conquer the most stubborn spots.

Clay and plastic pots are available in an array of sizes, from "thumb"—about an inch across the top—to 18 inches or more, and in three basic shapes:

1) The *standard,* as tall as it is wide across the top; for deep-rooted, tall plants.

2) The *azalea* or *three-quarter* is three-fourths as tall as it is wide; besides azalea, this configuration suits a wide variety of flowering and foliage plants and makes a serviceable all-purpose pot.

3) The *bulb pan, half pot* or *squatty pot* is half as tall as it is wide, and is used for shallow-rooted plants such as African violet, trailing rhizomatous begonia and spring bulbs being forced into winter bloom.

It is better not to plant in containers having no provision for drainage. The purpose of one or more drain holes is not only to drain off excess water, but also to permit air to reach the roots. Plants that are fertilized regularly also need to be flushed periodically with water only, a wellness treatment that is not possible in a drainless container.

Which pot for this plant?

Experience is the best teacher for fitting pots and plants. What looks right tends to work in terms of cultural needs, and vice versa. The rule of thumb I use is this: let the size of the pot equal one-half to one-third the height or width of the plant, depending on whether it is primarily vertical or horizontal. This suggests a 6-inch pot for an angel-wing begonia

Here is the ultimate in containers. Located at the Sun Yat-sen Memorial Hall in China it contains a fishtail palm (Caryota mitis).

PERLITE

VERMICULITE

PREPARED
MIX

Rooting test using miniature rose cuttings planted in three different materials. Longest roots and best top growth with perlite followed by cutting in vermiculite and last, the commercial mix which seems to stay too wet.

12 to 18 inches tall, a 4-inch pot for an African violet that measures 8 inches across.

When to repot

It is time to repot when roots fill the pot. This often coincides with the plant's having become top-heavy in relation to the pot. When this occurs during a period of active growth, transfer to a size or two larger pot but disturb the existing rootball as little as possible; add fresh potting mix as necessary to fill.

Complete repotting, in which most of the old growing medium is worked free of the roots and discarded, and a portion of the root system is pruned away, is done at the beginning of a season of active growth. Juvenile plants are typically given a complete repotting yearly; mature specimens may require repotting only every two or three years.

Top-dressing is one way to rejuvenate a plant without complete repotting. This technique works especially well for specimen trees or shrubs in large containers. Late winter and spring are perhaps the best times. Moisten the soil a day or two in advance. Use your fingers to loosen and remove the top 2 to 3 inches of old soil; use a large spoon or trowel to remove more of the old soil around the edges, between the rootball and the wall of the container. Refill with new potting.

Potting mix ingredients

Most of us who grow houseplants are aware, at least subconsciously, that their care constitutes beneficial therapy. Watering, misting, grooming, fertilizing, staking—all these activities are positive ways to relax, to spend quality time. They help me get wound up in the morning and unwind at night.

One of the most therapeutic aspects of growing plants is mixing potting soil. Psychiatric studies show that the farther removed we are from the earth, figuratively or in reality, the greater is our need for living plants and all they represent. If you've ever smelled freshly plowed soil on a warm spring day, you know it is one of the most exhilarating of all scents. When you mix some potting soil for your plants, you can experience this same sensation.

Since it is possible to buy all kinds of different potting soils pre-mixed for specific kinds of plants, you may wonder why I suggest doing it yourself. One reason is that working your hands in the varied textures of different ingredients is highly satisfying. The other is that by adding certain ingredients to packaged mixes you can get better growth responses.

For example, the typical packaged all-purpose potting soil, sometimes labeled for foliage plants, is too dense. I usually mix two to three parts of this with one to two parts of coarse vermiculite, which is also available in packages where plants are sold.

When I want to repot a flowering plant such as an African violet I start with a packaged soil labeled either for African violets or flowering houseplants. To two parts of this I add one part each of vermiculite and sphagnum peat moss. The vermiculite helps retain moisture but also allows air to reach the roots. Sphagnum peat moss provides valuable humus and assures proper acidity. A potting mix like this works well for most flowering houseplants—African violet, gloxinia, begonia and gardenia, to name a few.

If I am going to repot a cactus or other succulent such as kalanchoe, echeveria or jade plant *(Crassula),* I start with a packaged mix labeled for cactus. To four parts of this I add one part each of vermiculite and sphagnum peat moss. The reason I do this is that most packaged soil mixes for cacti dry out too quickly and become hard as concrete.

The fascinating thing about mixing your own potting soils is that you can start with almost any packaged mix and make it suitable for whatever plant you want to grow. For instance, to alter all-purpose or foliage plant potting soil for a flowering plant, start with two parts of it and add one part each of ver-

Don't forget the unusual when selecting containers. Japanese bonsai pots are suitable for many miniature plants such as Sinningia 'Dollbaby' *planted in a two and one-half inch pot.*

miculite and sphagnum peat moss. For cacti and other succulents use two parts all-purpose potting soil, two parts clean sharp sand (you can substitute perlite, available in bags where plants are sold, but never use sand from the seashore as it is too salty) and one-half part each of vermiculite and sphagnum peat moss.

If you have access to garden soil or well-rotted compost, you can use it in place of the packaged potting soil, ideally not before it has been put through a quarter-inch mesh screen and pasteurized in the oven at 180 °F for 30 minutes to an hour. Instead of vermiculite— or in addition to—you can use well-rotted leaf mold, also screened and pasteurized; this is especially good for begonias, gesneriads and philodendrons, in particular the self-headers such as *P. selloum* and *P. wendlandii.* In my book there is no substitute for sphagnum peat moss; the dark, powdery kinds do not have the bulk, the fibrous, spongy nature needed to aerate the soil in a pot—today or a year from now.

How much to water

This is a complicated subject, but here let's be simplistic and think in terms of three basic conditions, dry, evenly moist and wet. *Dry* suggests a plant that requires watering well and then not again until the top half inch of soil feels dry to your fingers. Any plant in the dry category will suffer from having its pot stand in a saucer of excess water for more

than an hour. *Evenly moist* describes what most plants need. Water well. An hour or two later pour off any water remaining in the saucer. When a pinch of the surface soil feels barely damp to your fingers, but before it feels really dry, water well again. *Wet* constantly is a condition required by few houseplants. Chinese evergreen (*Aglaonema*) doesn't mind, but it also seems to do just as well evenly moist. *Cyperus* needs to be wet, and of course the aquatics love water so much they live in it.

It is impossible to suggest how often and how much you will have to water any given plant in order to maintain its moisture preference. There are too many variables. Plants growing actively in good light and warm temperatures will require more water than those growing in poor light or coolness. Plants

Potting mix ingredients: Left to right, from top row: White marble chips for drainage and mulch, golden colored vermiculite or exploded mica, granulated hardwood charcoal. Row Two: fir bark chips for potting epiphytes, mulching and mixtures for semi-terrestrial plants, unmilled sphagnum moss. Third row: chunks of hardwood charcoal for drainage, white volcanic rock (medium grade perlite, mixture of peat moss and perlite (Peatlite). Bottom row: broken clay pots or crocks, sphagnum peatmoss, Baccto potting soil.

automated to the extent that they receive only electric light of the same intensity and duration day after day also tend to require more water—and fertilizer—than those solely dependent on the whims of the weather and window light.

There is one steadfast rule about watering houseplants: they respond best to water of room temperature or slightly warmer, tepid or lukewarm to the touch.

Fertilizing houseplants

With all the variables, this gets so complicated that for most plants I say simply *while in active growth*. Of course, some plants will be unable to grow actively until you fertilize. During the cooler average temperatures and shorter days of fall and early winter, houseplants in window light need little or no fertilizer. Frequent applications of dilute fertilzer give better results than infrequent, heavy doses. In any event, read the product label.

Shopping for Soil

Dirt, in case you haven't noticed, is not dirt-cheap, at least not at the rate of $2 for four quarts (4.4 liters), which is what I paid recently at a plant shop in my neighborhood. At another, only a few blocks away, I found the same quantity of potting soil for half the price.

The front of the $2 bag promised potting soil "scientifically improved and expertly blended; weed free and ready to use." The word "organic" also appeared. The dollar bag claimed to contain "all-organic potting soil; sterilized; expertly blended. Will not cake."

The back of the $2 bag described its contents as a "scientific blend of compost, peat, perlite and humus, all mixed to a uniform consistency." For half the money I was offered a "scientifically balanced formula combining the proper amounts of quality soil, rich humus and organic additives."

Having read the labels, I next opened both bags, felt the soil with my fingers and then examined it with a magnifying glass. As nearly as I could tell, they were exactly the same, one simply cost twice what the other did.

At the same time I also purchased a two-quart bag of soil labeled "African Violet Mix," for $1.19. It offered a "balance of peat, organic compost, bark and humus combined with porous rock and conditioners. Correct pH is assured." On examination I detected some "porous rock," probably perlite, otherwise the mix appeared exactly the same as those sold simply as "potting soil."

A bag marked "Cactus Mix," and also "guaranteed not to cake or pack," cost me $2 for four quarts of a "scientifically prepared blend of sterile sand, vermiculite and firm soil as well as the right amount of natural growth elements." Label promises also included "sterilized, non-burning, expertly blended, odorless," the last being disappointing since I consider the smell of healthy soil highly desirable.

Fortunately, when I opened the bag the pleasant aroma one expects from living soil was present. Examination of the mix itself showed more sand than the others but no vermiculite and not, in my opinion, enough humus for a potting mix described as "ideal for all cacti, as well as succulents and all bulbs."

Besides the obvious, that it pays to comparison shop, the conclusions I've drawn where convenience potting mixes are concerned are these:

1) Labels offer only a hint of actual content. "Peat," for example; is it the powdery, brown-black kind that is of little value or that wondrous, fibrous, spongy, reddish-brown sphagnum peat moss that is universally recommended for potting mixes and general soil improvement?

2) The words "expert" and "blend" have little meaning until you've proven them true in your own environment and with your own watering and fertilizing habits. The mixes I sampled seemed also to have been screened so finely that "blend" took on negative connotations, as if the ingredients had been put through some giant processor that reduced every particle to the size of a tiny grain of sand.

3) Most packaged potting soils are best used as one ingredient in mixtures "blended expertly" by your own hands—for the specific kinds of plants you are about to pot. This saves money, gives better results and lets you enjoy more time in beneficial physical contact with the soil.

Potting Mix Recipes

Time-honored All-purpose Potting Soil

1 part garden loam or packaged all-purpose potting soil
1 part sphagnum peat moss
1 part perlite or clean, sharp sand

For African violet, Chinese hibiscus, gardenia, other flowering types: add an extra portion of sphagnum peat moss.

For cacti and other succulents from dry regions: add an extra portion of perlite or sand.

Cornell Peat-Lite Mix A

For one bushel of mix, good for seeds or repotting plants:
4 gallons #2 or #3 horticultural vermiculite
4 gallons shredded sphagnum peat moss
2 level tablespoons dolomite limestone (do not use hydrated or "quick" lime)
2 level tablespoons 20 percent superphosphate
2 level tablespoons potassium nitrate *or* calcium nitrate

Add one pint warm water to the peat moss to moisten. Put all ingredients into a large plastic bag; inflate by blowing into the end. Twist closed to keep inflated. Now shake, roll and tumble the contents to mix well. Use at once or store in the bag.

Fertilizer added at mixing will last for three weeks of growth, then it will be necessary to fertilize regularly using a water-soluble fertilizer such as 20-20-20.

Cornell Epiphytic Mix

For one bushel of mix that may be used for aroids (aglaonema, dieffenbachia, scindapsus, philodendron), bromeliads, cacti, orchids, peperomia:
⅓ bushel sphagnum peat moss
⅓ bushel medium grade horticultural perlite
⅓ bushel Douglas, red or white fir bark (1/8-1/4" size)
8 level tablespoons dolomite limestone
6 tablespoons 20 percent superphosphate
3 tablespoons 10-10-10 fertilizer
1 tablespoon potassium nitrate
3 tablespoons granular wetting agent

Control of Pests and Diseases

Notes from Guest Editor

Charles Marden Fitch

From time to time even the best cared for indoor plants will suffer from pest attacks or diseases such as mildew or rot. Pests are often introduced with newly acquired plants. I have a standing joke about a few careless commercial nurseries that they give you free mealybugs with every purchase!

Most commercial growers try to keep their plants free from pests yet the pests are just as eager to infest their favorite foods. Here are some suggestions for keeping your indoor plants healthy.

1) Before buying plants, inspect them for obvious signs of pests or disease. Don't buy specimens that look sick or are infested with pests.

2) Isolate new plants from your established collection for several weeks. During this time watch for pests that may appear from hatching eggs or the soil. Pesticide sprays frequently kill adults but not the eggs or underground pests.

3) Create a healthy environment around your plants. Provide adequate air circulation to discourage mold, rots, and mildew. Furnish adequate humidity and water early in the day so leaves are dry by nightfall.

4.) When you find a problem, take immediate action. Mildew and rot spread quickly and

Soft brown scale insects can be seen along the center stem of this Boston fern. Tiny white specks seen on the leaflets are young scale insects. The regularly spaced light brown dots along the top of each leaflet are normal sori which release reproductive spores of fern.

Water resting in the center of this Aloe polyphylla *started rot which finally killed the plant.*

insects spread to nearby plants. If you are unsure of the cause of the problem take an affected plant to a nearby expert for help. Garden centers, plant shops, garden club members, county agricultural agents, botanical gardens, university botany/agricultural departments are all places that will usually provide diagnostic assistance.

5) Treat pests and diseases with appropriate remedies. Local garden centers and nurseries usually offer products designed to control specific problems. For maximum personal safety use products approved for indoor application.

6) Discard plants with terminal problems. If a plant is covered with scale or almost dead from rot it is better to get rid of the specimen and start anew with a healthy plant.

Pests

The most troublesome pests for indoor plants and suggested treatments follow:
Aphids: Wash off the pests with warm soapy water (SAFER Insecticidal soap or Ivory).
Caterpillars: Pick off and throw out these chewing pests. I feed them to my carnivorous *Nepenthes.*

Sometimes insecticides which are safe for house-plants may cause flower damage as can be seen on this African violet. The foliage has not been damaged.

Aphids suck sap from Hedera *'Curlilocks.' Shed skins of the insects are seen on the leaf below the ivy stem encrusted with fat gray aphids.*

Mealybugs: Pick off all exposed clumps.
Mites: Red spider mites are common on thin-leaved plants under dry sunny conditions. Wash plants under lukewarm water.
Scale: Scrape off all accessible scales. Wash plants with soapy water (Ivory or SAFER Insecticidal Soap).
Whiteflies: Spray with insecticidal soap every three to five days.

Rots and Mildew

Discourage root rot by letting soil dry slightly between watering. For dampoff of seedlings and new cuttings use a drench of Banrot or similar product offered in garden stores for treating soil and potting mixes to control dampoff rots. Many rots and fungus problems spread by splashing water and using unclean cutting tools. Keep your collection free of diseased leaves. Flame sterilize cutting tools between use on different plants, avoid overhead watering where mildew and leaf rots are a problem. Keep a fan going all the time to encourage air circulation around the plants. Rots, fungus, mildew flourish in still moist air.

Basic information about...

Houseplants Under Lights

Charles Marden Fitch

Renanthopsis *Fiery Gem has a compact growth habit and peach-red flowers peppered with darker spots.*

Using fluorescent lights to supplement daylight or to create indoor light gardens gives one freedom to grow houseplants almost anywhere. Some of my most beautiful tropicals are grown in the basement under fluorescent lamps. When the plants are at their blooming best they are given display space in the living room, on a dining room table or in a similar prominent location. Such a system lets me utilize space in an already heated, easily accessible place where I only have to provide adequate light and humidity.

Friends of mine have built virtual greenhouses in their basements, thus having no trouble from storms, cloudy days, extra cold weather—or excessively high heating bills. Even more exciting are attractive light gardens designed to be a decorative part of an indoor living area. For example, a feature of my own living room is a wall-mounted light garden kept in good condition by a combination of early morning sunlight and three 40-watt fluorescent lamps. This particular unit is made by a commercial firm (Marko Company) specifically as a light garden that will fit into decorated interiors while still providing sufficient illumination for sturdy growth of flowering houseplants. It is forty-eight inches long and twelve inches high, a size quite compatible with the average room.

Light gardens in living areas, as contrasted perhaps with those in spare rooms or the basement, should be designed as attractive features where plants can be seen at their best. To avoid glare from the lamps a wedged louver can be used just under the fixture. A louver with a waffle-type pattern of holes

Fluorescent self-standing fixture has two 20-watt lamps. Plants grown under broad spectrum fluorescent tubes are left to right: Rex begonia 'Shirt Sleeves,' Chirita sinensis, Ficus pumila minima. *In the back is red dwarf orchid* Sophrolaeliocattleya *Tiger Eye, and* Pelargonium *'Little Gem'. The mirror foil beneath the Mexican pottery reflects light and duplicates the scene.*

permits most of the lamp light to fall directly upon the plants but will prevent direct viewing of the bulbs from the side or above. Some manufacturers offer indoor light gardens already equipped with these wedged louvers. You may also obtain the louver material for use in custom-made light gardens in hardware stores.

Several portable light gardens resembling furniture are offered in catalogs and at garden shops. Those with only one or two lamps are suitable for foliage plants and certain flowering subjects with low-light requirements such as African violets, especially if the light garden can be placed where plants receive some supplemental daylight.

Light garden carts with two to four tiers, each carrying a waterproof shelf under an efficient fixture, are very practical for growing plants in a limited space. Although the basic design of the tiered light gardens is more functional than decorative, one can cus-tomize these units to suit personal taste. For example, I didn't like the shiny metal on one of my tiered units, but a can of metal paint let me change the impression immediately. Vines and trailing plants can be effectively used to soften the edges and hide unattractive features of a light garden. One might also build a shell or false front to enclose the functional tiered light garden.

Whatever the design, one must allow for adequate air circulation. Except for propagating cabinets where a constant high temperature might be an advantage, the usual light garden should be kept between 60° and 75°F. Since the ballasts required for fluorescent lamps generate heat, there must always be some way for this heat to escape. If a light garden is enclosed, provision must be made for ventilation, such as an open top or drilling a number of holes (perhaps in decorative shapes) around the base or sides of a cabinet.

Humidity

Extra humidity can be furnished in a light garden by growing plants on moist perlite or gravel. Roots will escape through the container drainage holes, however, making re-arrangement of the pots difficult after a few months. Such outside rooting can be prevented if pots are placed on saucers or a

wedged louver above the moist material. In fact, with truly waterproof trays under the plants one can keep an inch or two of water in the tray, then place pots on a wooden or wire grid above this miniature "lake." Normal evaporation of the water will furnish extra humidity. Caution: plant roots should never be waterlogged.

Exacum affine 'Midget' (back) and Peperomia *'Little Fantasy' GROWN UNDER THREE DIFFERENT SOURCES OF fluorescent light show marked variations in plant habit. Plants grew fastest under Wide Spectrum Gro-Lux and also bloomed well. The most compact growth but fewer flowers occurred under standard rosy-hued Gro-Lux. The Vita-Lite lamps are the same color as sunlight.*

Light Choice

Indoor plants will grow under all of the commonly available fluorescent lamps. If natural color is very important, as in a dining room, you may want to use lamps that have a color similar to noon sunlight. Among such kinds are GE Chroma-50, Vita-Lite and Verilux, which are broad-spectrum lamps. Cacti and orchids are some of the high-light-requirement plants that thrive under broad-spectrum lamps, provided that intensity is adequate.

For slightly warm tones, but an excellent spectrum for plants that are grown for their flowers, choose one of the horticultural broad-spectrum lamps such as Agro-Lite or Wide Spectrum Gro-Lux. These are more expensive than common household lamps such as cool white and warm white, but they furnish a better spectrum of light for those plants which grow better under such illumination.

Most foliage plants and African violets will do perfectly well under a combination of one cool white and one warm white fluorescent lamp, so if budget is an important factor you will want to choose these least expensive lamps for such plants.

A "theatrical" impression is created by Gro-Lux lamps, the first and most famous horticultural lamps. Standard Gro-Lux lamps cost more than the Wide Spectrum Gro-Lux, but they are the only ones that have a deep pink color. The warm-colored light makes flower and leaf color glow. Rex begonias and African violets look spectacular under standard Gro-Lux lamps, as do red-toned orchids. Plants grow compactly under them, too.

Distance and Other Points

High-light-requirement plants such as most orchids, succulents and bromeliads look best with foliage two to six inches under the lamps. Keeping the plants too far away means that the light may be too dim for maximum flower production and compact growth. Houseplants with lower light requirements, such as foliage plants, rex begonias and African violets, will thrive ten to fifteen inches under two to four lamps. Since light diminishes at the ends of fluorescent lamps, it is more efficient to use the longest lamp possible, rather than put two smaller lamps end-to-end.

84

For plants with high-light requirements, provide a minimum of four lamps per fixture for optimum growth and flowering. My basement fixtures each have four 40-watt lamps. For orchids and succulents I use all four, but for foliage plants and African violets I use only two. Plants given too much light grow compactly, may not display flowers correctly and often have a sickly yellow appearance. Plants given too little light intensity will lose character by growing spindly and elongated, lack color or turn very dark green. Plants provided with the correct intensity look well balanced, have the color and shape characteristic of the species and display flowers without having unduly elongated stems.

The best way to time light-garden hours is with an automatic timer to turn the fixtures on and off, according to your program. Most houseplants grow well with a fourteen to sixteen hour day. In the winter one might set the timer to provide an eleven to twelve hour day, which is required by a few plants such as rhizomatous begonias if they are to bloom. After two months of short days (eleven hours) begin a long-day cycle again, so that by spring the light garden is receiving fourteen to sixteen hours of light.

Learn More

Detailed suggestions concerning this subject, plus designs for several indoor light gardens, will be found in *The Complete Book of Houseplants Under Lights* (Charles Marden Fitch, Hawthorne Books), available at most libraries. Some of the lamp manufacturers, such as Duro Test (Vita-Lite) and Sylvania (Gro-Lux), offer free folders with light garden suggestions.

If you wish to learn more about this kind of gardening write to the Indoor Gardening Society of America, c/o Horticultural Society of New York, 128 West 58th St., New York, NY 10019. The Society has many local chapters where members are pleased to provide personal advice. The bimonthly magazine always has several articles for beginning light gardeners, plus useful addresses for light garden supplies.

Floral cart with the exterior of reflectors painted. Pots rest on moist gravel.

Some Mail Order Sources
For Indoor Plants and Seeds

Firms:	Specialities/Catalog:

Abbey Gardens
4620 Carpinteria Ave.
Carpinteria
CA 93013

Cacti and other
succulents.
Catalog $2.00

Alberts & Merkel Bros., Inc.
2210 S. Federal Highway
Boynton Beach
FL 33435

Aroids, bromeliads.
Free list to Plant
Society members.

Altman Specialty Plants
553 Buena Creek Rd.
San Marcos
CA 92069

Cacti and unusual
succulents.
Catalog $1.00

W. Atlee Burpee Co.
300 Park Ave.
Warminster
PA 18974

Seeds and plants of
popular house-
plants. Catalog
free.

California EPI Center
P.O. Box 1431
Vista
CA 92083

Epiphytic cacti,
hoyas.
Catalog $1.00

Gesneriad Research Foundation
1873 Oak St.
Sarasota
FL 33577

Unusual gesneriads.
Send stamped self-
addressed envelope
for current list.

Glasshouse Works
Box 97
Stewart
OH 45778

Aroids, gesneriads,
foliage, succulents.
Catalog $1.50

Kartuz Greenhouses
1408 Sunset Drive
Vista
CA 92083

Begonias, ges-
neriads, other rare
exotics. Catalog
$2.00

Lauray of Salisbury
Undermountain Rd.
Salisbury
CT 06068

Begonias, ges-
nariads, succulents.
Catalog $1.75

Logee's Greenhouses
55 North St.
Danielson
CT 06239

Most exotic plants,
especially begonias
and geraniums.
Catalog $3.00

Merry Gardens
Camden
ME 04843

Foliage, geraniums,
begonias.
Catalog $1.00

Mini-Roses
P.O. Box 4255 Sta. A
Dallas
TX 75208

Miniature roses.
Catalog free.

Nor'East Miniature Roses
58 Hammond St.
Rowley
MA 01969

Miniature roses.
Catalog free.

Geo. W. Park Co.
P.O. Box 31
Greenwood
SC 29647

Seeds and plants of
many indoor
plants. Catalog free.

The Plant Kingdom
Att. Patrick Worley
Box 7273
Lincoln Acres
CA 92047

Hybridizer of
begonias and ges-
neriads. Many un-
usual exotic plants.
Catalog $1.00

Rainbow Gardens
P.O. Box 721
La Habra
CA 90631

Epiphytic cacti,
hoyas.
Catalog $1.00

Rhapis Gardens
100 Rhapis Rd.
P.O. Box 287
Gregory
TX 78359

Rhapis palms, rare
cultivars.
Catalog $1.00

Rosehill Farm
Gregg Neck Road, Box 406
Galena
MD 21635

Miniature roses.
Catalog free.

Sequoia Nursery
2519 E. Noble Ave.
Visalia
CA 93227

Miniature roses.
Catalog free.

Thompson & Morgan Seedsmen
P.O. Box 1308
Jackson
NJ 08527

Seeds of most
exotic houseplants.
Catalog free.

Tropiflora
2570 Tallevast Rd.
Sarasota
FL 34243

Bromeliads.
List $2.00 includes
credit coupon for
order.

Plant Society Lists

African Violet Society of
America
P.O. Box 3609
Beaumont
TX 77704

Illustrated magazine.
Shows.

American Begonia Society
P.O. Box 502
Encinitas
CA 92024

Illustrated magazine.
Shows/convention.

American Gloxinia &
Gesneriad Society
P.O. Box 493
Beverly Farms
MA 01915

Illustrated magazine.
Convention/show.

American Orchid Society
Inc.
6000 South Olive Ave.
West Palm Beach
FL 33405

Illustrated magazine.
Monthly judging in
18 regional centers.

The American Plant Life
Society
P.O. Box 985
National City
CA 92050

Journal of bulbous
plants such as the
amaryllis family.

The Bromeliad Society, Inc.
2488 E. 49th
Tulsa
OK 74105

Illustrated magazine.
Shows/convention.

Cactus and Succulent
Society
2631 Fairgreen Ave.
Arcadia
CA 91006

Illustrated magazine.
Shows.

The Cryptanthus Society
2355 Rusk
Beaumont
TX 77702

Publication, advice.

Gesneriad Research
Foundation
1873 Oak St.
Sarasota
FL 33577

Bulletin, rare plant
offerings, research.

Hoya Society International
P.O. Box 54271
Atlanta
GA 30308

Illustrated bulletin.

Indoor Citrus & Rare Fruit
Society
176 Coronado Ave.
Los Altos
CA 94022

Publication, advice.

Indoor Gardening Society
of America Inc.
128 W. 58th St.
New York
NY 10019

Publication, show.

International Aroid Society
Inc.
P.O. Box 43-1853
South Miami
FL 33143

Journal, shows.

Maximum-minimum thermometer will provide precise information on the high and low temperatures in any area.

The plant society groups listed here are often run by dedicated volunteers. From time to time an address may change when the membership secretary changes. The most current society address will be found in the society publications, available at botanical garden libraries. When writing for membership information enclose a self-addressed stamped envelope.

Join a plant society to receive the publication, participate in round robin letters, learn more about growing your favorite plants. Some of the plant societies have seed funds, local chapters, and yearly conventions.

C.M.F.

THE EYE THAT DESIRES
TO LOOK UPWARD

THE EYE THAT DESIRES
TO LOOK UPWARD

Poems by

Steven Cramer

THE GALILEO PRESS LTD

Baltimore, Maryland

ACKNOWLEDGMENTS

Some of these poems, or earlier versions of them, originally appeared in the following periodicals and anthologies:

The Agni Review: "Head of a Young Girl," "My Accomplished Friend," "The Narcissus," "Poem from a Balcony," "Self-Portrait with a City Background"
Anthology of Magazine Verse: "Two Women with Mangoes"
Antioch Review: "Ailanthus," "To Francis Jammes"
Bay Windows: "The Paradise Cafe"
The Boston Review: "Provincetown, October," "Etude"
Crazy Horse: "The Woman on the Beach"
Cutbank: "Two Women with Mangoes"
The Iowa Review: "Bitter Exercise"
The Nation: "Uncle in Sunshine"
The Ohio Review: "Thirty-Three and a Third," "The Youngest Son"
Partisan Review: "For Now"
Pequod: "Mercy," "The Present Tense"
Ploughshares: "Aix-en-Provence," "Freud's Desk, Vienna, 1938," "Homage to C. P. Cavafy," "Letter from Boston, Patriot's Day"
Poetry: "Pentimento"
Seattle Review: "Manasquan"
Seneca Review: "Garlic"
Sonora Review: "Marie's Snow"

I am grateful to the Artists Foundation of the Massachusetts Council on the Arts and Humanities for a fellowship awarded in 1983, and to the National Endowment for the Arts for a grant awarded in 1984, both of which were helpful to me in completing this book.

Finally, my deep gratitude to Stuart Dischell, Marie Howe, Gail Mazur, Askold Melnyczuk, Ira Sadoff, Thomas Swiss, and Stephen Tapscott for their advice and encouragement.

Published by The Galileo Press, Ltd., 15201 Wheeler Lane, Sparks, Maryland 21152

Typography by Capitol Communication Systems, Crofton, Maryland. Printing and perfect binding by The Sheridan Press, Hanover, Pennsylvania. Case binding by Murphy-Parker, Inc., Philadelphia, Pennsylvania.

Publication of this book was made possible in part by grants from the National Endowment for the Arts and from the Maryland State Arts Council.

This book has been typeset in Garamond Light.

Cover art: "Baumstudie, 1885–90," by Paul Cézanne. Reprinted with permission of the Kunsthaus, Zürich.

Cover design by Jack Stephens

ISBN 0-913123-10-2 (cloth)
ISBN 0-913123-11-0 (paper)

Library of Congress Catalog Card Number 86-82444

First Edition

For Pernel Berkeley

CONTENTS

I

II

III

For we are like tree trunks in the snow. In appearance they lie sleekly and a little push should be enough to set them rolling. No, it can't be done, for they are firmly wedded to the ground. But see, even that is only appearance.

—Franz Kafka
"Meditation"

I

For Now

This morning letting the trees stand
over the unappeasable man I've become,
I'm loitering in an unused backyard plot,
afraid a neighbor might lift up a shade
and recognize me and remain unmoved,
certain I've let my nature grow
brittle and veined, skin of a leaf
stretched over a stone, the muddy reek
of last night's rain drying, and the air
inside me dusty as the air inside a tent;
and feeling ridiculous and skittish
with this mortal look on my face,
I rub my thumb across the bark,
follow the limbs that divide and turn
invisible, each pointing out a new ambiguity
the longer I look; and I look to my windows,
three black boxes housing my absence now,
and above them the late-August sky, white
as water churned by someone's hand; then out
through a weedy gap in the wire fence,
a teenage couple shortcuts from nowhere
to nowhere, stops—the girl touching
the boy's shoulder, lightly, for balance,
shaking a stone or twig from her shoe,
then both walking on as if to prove
nothing is random or unasked for, even
this startling morning we've stumbled into:
the only one, for now, we know.

Marie's Snow

Then you rushed to the window,
an ardent astronomer

checking the pulse of novas,
as though projecting your eyes

were the trick of a light-
year's leap. A moment before,

we'd been at it again—
defining, that is, who we are

and whether or not we were
perfect. We weren't

so magnetic and distant
as stars, and nowhere near

as attractive, though you looked
awfully good on my floor,

legs crossed and hands
palming a facet of crystal,

mined from Mount Ida,
which I'll compare us to,

because it is nicked, prismatic;
picks up lint from pockets;

and especially because
so easily misplaced. No,

too pointed a figure—
even more a pebble we stumble

upon, worry and toss,
a momentary fit for the palm

shaped for it. Then you rushed
to the window, and below

the snow rose in loaves
on the steps, spines on branches,

feathery down on the rooftops,
on the hoods and trunks of cars

weaving the streets like floes,
on the shoulders of a man

you pointed out, who appeared
to be speaking, arguing

with the watermarks of salt
on his shoes. Of course

we heard nothing quite
so remote, but why not

let the shortfall of words
cover space? If I make it

your snow, however unlikely
we'll improve upon it,

I'll never have to do
without your voice—

how it spirited us
down the four flights

into the snow's blue light,
which softened each consonant,

lengthened each vowel, and rose
in the steam of our webbed breath.

Two Women with Mangoes

One seems to offer her breasts
as if they were fruit, though she holds
the canoe-shaped bowl of mangoes like a gift
received. Her eyes dart off to the right,
one hand curving around the bowl's rim
as though to guard what it presents.
The other woman holds a small bouquet
of pinkish-white flowers, presses them
between her palms. In that green dress
exposing only one breast,
she looks more chaste than her friend.
Is it correct to call them friends?
Certainly the wash of green and yellow
in the background is not friendly—
turbulent weather or a growth of weeds.
If these women and their island
offer nothing we could need, then what
should we ask for?
                        Gauguin, at 17,
joined the navy, traveled to Brazil.
When he left his wife, five children
and Impressionism for Tahiti,
he must have been aroused by what he found
at first—the coppery skin, bodies uncorseted.
But these women don't look like lovers.
If the fruit they hold, the breasts they show,
are presents to give, they're not for us;
we don't know what to ask for.
Perhaps their pose was Gauguin's own
rendition of two women, two refusals—
the head of one turned slightly toward the other,
as if she were about to speak, or had just spoken.

The Question

She asked if sheer joy
made the gulls hover. Ignorant
as kites, they delayed above our blanket
while the waves bridled and slurred.
And farther out, beyond the boats
idling on their tethers, haze
lent the sea a sun-struck gloss.

The question stuck. A wave pulled back,
puzzling the beach with furrowed shells.
And I wonder if that's why we stopped
following the water, caught
ankle-deep between three elements,
our aching feet knuckling deeper in.

The gulls called down their vocables
of doubt, told fortunes I couldn't fathom.
And she felt it too, I could tell—
as the eyes squint at the world's quiz,
the mind relies on paraphrase. In other words,
I could have said yes, I could have agreed

that from each loitering gull shadow
healing distillates could be pressed,
that we might peel their silhouettes off
the beach, keep them airborne forever.
But she'd already gone in, lost
then found in the vacillating swells,
answering me with her hand's sure wave.

Uncle in Sunshine

A long time now he's been making those trips
to Florida, to the dog races,
at the earliest sign of winter.
Relaxing with his canaries on a veranda
overlooking the beach, he watches children
reassemble the starched bones of fish.
Daylight cares for the middle-aged, he says;
clear water is what moves him.

But each winter he brings in
a little less. The odds disappoint him.
There's an insistence, now, in the rasp
of leaves across a macadam road.
Feverish winds blow down from the Carolinas,
a plague like the plagues in Venice.
Is he part of a sexual myth,
trials of the hero bound to a mast?
And the gulls—are they sirens
returned to earth to tempt him with their phrases?

Women sit near him in the restaurant
with dried, doll-faces that melt in the heat.
Overhead, parakeets brood in their cages,
taking care of themselves, speaking
among themselves: one of the more
irritating sounds of this world.
A long time now he's been taking those walks
through the generous sunlight. . . .

Uncle, it's the sea you think about these days,
ironic cries for help, radios broadcasting
Brooklyn accents and the steady baritone of waves.
There must be some way to untangle these sounds,
these isolated voices in a fugue.

Self-Portrait with a City Background

The sun, as it sets, seems to leave
a veneer of light across each window.

He stands looking out, hands on the sill,
while an indistinct scent returns
with dusk—pine needles, mint.
An excellent evening, he hopes,
will settle over the rows of wooden houses,
over the bus depots. And he hopes
a breeze will drift in from the Atlantic,
carrying a little cool mist, but no rain.

Because, this evening, his friends are away,
he thinks: *here's a city in which we could live,*
here's an avenue where we'll meet as planned,
here are the redemptive letters . . .

Sometimes the retiring world is miraculous,
a charade so disarming
it shames him into concentration:
the definite source of that fragrance
held just short of remembrance, the tilting
red flowers in the living room below.
And just before sleep, in his best thoughts,
he watches the street relax into night,
where an ordinary rain is falling.

Etude

Theoretical as particles of light,
these notes perfect their course,

piano, through a neighbor's open window.
They don't resemble stones

dropped in water, or the flywheel
of a spindle, or a spirit's

fingerprints. They won't be pictured.
In rough counterpoint,

my face looms in the shaving mirror,
estranged as the day moon,

so fixed by gravity
I see guidewires around the eyes,

no matter how much I shear away
or wish it clean. Now and then

the focus deepens, as in a telescope,
when a mote of light, at first

a nameless star, sharpens into Saturn.
Ringed with luminous dust,

it drifts past the lens's field
of vision—so swiftly!—

you'd think the world had turned
away its gaze. I might never see

the one who spins that music,
the one whose gifted satellites

run rings around my study.
If perfection is invisible,

at times we are allowed to glimpse
its schedule; like another planet's

performance, virtuoso,
it lends brief proof of the earth.

Aix-en-Provence

April 1975

On another side of the world,
vendors hawk skinned rabbits, olives
peppered with the dust of cheese.
And each of their streetside stalls
opens at dawn, closes at dusk—
flowers, sea urchins, mussels.

So the memory of one foreign city
opens, reappears from a journal
left neglected in a drawer, the need
to record a shaft of afternoon light.
It's the same light I remember sharpening
the animal smells of the marketplace

as I first walked those narrow streets:
farmers with skin the texture of canvas,
their wives stacking grapes into pyramids.
And my friend, my interpreter,
you counted my coins into their hands,
sweet tufted fruit, bread and watercress.

For a month the mistral blew,
slate clattered down our roof,
collected in gutters, doors unlatched.
Some days we woke to a world underwater,
trees swaying like gulfweed, fish-shaped leaves
plastered against the windows. In this change

in the world, what was magical?
Or is memory a sourceless chronicle?
Although I remember your name, I'd prefer
to hear those supple inflections again,
see you turn from the cutting board, sleeves rolled,
your hands chafed and stained with all they made.

The Present Tense

Suppose you could see from beyond
these coppery bricks, these rooftop gardens
with their thin, exiled rows of vegetables—
the city would then appear fixed
in motion, a gesture drawing.

But as each day grows shorter,
streets are themselves and the earth
below them, layer on layer
of footprints and chance encounters.
And it's easier to notice
how changeable you've become.
From one moment to the next,
your body quivers in its sheath,
outmatched by traffic, then holds
your stilled mind, benched
in the emptiness of late afternoons.

And it's a fine thing to be
reminded of the avenue's randomness,
or the forces of weather that winnow
a piece of land to form a harbor.
But sometimes your name and address
brush against you like strangers
unbalanced by parcels, receding into a crowd—
no apology, no hint of recognition.

So protect yourself,
by watching from a fourth-floor window,

while snow adds another layer,
a mute, impermanent white, water and not water,
and for this moment believe yourself
constant, having nowhere to go
and no desire to return.

The Narcissus

When I turn my head
(away from whatever task
I belong to) and see the Narcissus
I placed on the window sill—
a gift from someone who thought me kind—
I don't mind the easy notion
that I look at myself, its name
welcomes the ease of such thinking.

Rooted in white gravel,
its twin bulbs are ugly as onions
or two graceless feet, leathery-looking.
But the thirty or more green stalks
spear up like the stems of lilies,
inviting the eye that desires
to look upward, to look upward.
And finally the flower,
which is not one flower but eleven
smaller blossoms gathered.

I think the Narcissus
admires its various selves:
the paper-bag brown of its first skin,
the stalks I count and recount,
the five petals joined
to make these eleven cut-paper stars—
centered in each a cup to hold
the core of orange pollen—
and the yellow-white cluster they fashion,
so dry to the touch it's a papery feeling.
To that wrinkled accumulation,

to that more or less the sum of its parts,
to that flower—my eye travels.

When I come home
from a day so ill-fitting
I want to forget what I look like,
having shied from any reflecting thing—
upended trees in a puddle
or the bus window's portrait of stasis—
this single Narcissus flower,
which multiplies its parts
the closer you look
and makes all counting uncanny,
has simply spent the day
turning on its neck to the light.

And I turn it away
from the window to face me.

II

For H.R.:

What can the spirit believe?—
It takes in the whole body;
I, on coming to love,
Make that my study.

          —Theodore Roethke

To Francis Jammes

In a manner, we all pray.

So I've walked out at 6 a.m.
into the sound and look of things.
Arc lamps hum in the city park,
and accepting resistance,
swallows lift in a sudden breeze.

What presses against me now?

Francis Jammes, you prayed to be simple,
prayed to enter heaven with the donkeys,
to have a simple wife.

On mornings like these,
insects sluggish in the cooling weather,
as fog pools in the narrow spaces
between houses—all common
for September—
I could say I have nothing.

You would say life resumed this morning.

The Woman on the Beach

with the near perfect body
understands us.
She knows the sure vanity of lying here
by a reservoir edged with brown foam.
The woman's bathing suit
is brown, and also our imaginings
are of a dark color:
the gravel was fine beneath the elms
where you approached me in a straw hat,
black ribbon stitched along its rim.
While children knee-deep in the shallows
slap the water into glassy fans,
we long for a painless tan
until it's too late, and all we can do is stand
carefully, without touching.
So each season offers a reflection
of our nervousness: these fingering rivulets
have their place to get to,
despite the wildness of the shore;
and the shore itself seems a vast, glacial tundra
where the wind makes us edgy and intelligent.
Maybe we were hoping for such desolation,
for now the cliffs sharpen against a cloudless sky,
rising up as we lie down;
and this placid version of water,
spotted with green and yellow rafts,
recedes. Waking up, we'll notice how the sand
has sifted into everything we own,
making abrasive everything we do. But surely
you're still sleeping, your arm right-angled

as a pillow while the crowd doubles.
Now if our bodies are mere decoration,
weathered by the sun, it's not yet
in the wiser sense of aging. Summer's absolute
while it lasts.
               I don't know if you're dreaming
or just thinking of the many routes I'll take to leave you.

The Tempest

The rain pelted our cabin roof
like wind-driven grains of sand, kept us
in and up. "We're weathering love's perils,"
I'd have said if we'd been speaking.
The ocean's scent came on strong,
took away our appetites, and no
salt taste revived us. We were drugged
on what we'd smuggled in this last-ditch
vacation: too much reminiscence,
the familiar chafe of your skin, my skin.

The storm broke the third night,
but we still needed shelter. In the film,
Prospero, post-modern architect,
fed cruel magic to the Mediterranean,
shipwrecked the estranged and released
their reconciliations. Our faces rinsed
colorless in the screen's glare,
we watched the masque take place
behind a curtain of ascending credits,
the illusion of surfacing, a last sea change . . .

Before I slipped into a patchwork sleep,
rising twice that night to sound your body,
diving back beneath some artless dream,
I heard the rocks hiss again
as the sea washed up the men and women,

beaching them like splintered skiffs.
When the wind's pitch finally eased,
when the sky returned its Grecian blue,
I stood on the wizard's cliff and watched,
allowing every cast-away, uncoupled body
the deep sleep of those who've run aground.

Bitter Exercise

Sit up, lie down, sit up, lie down, run
around and around the block

until a little of myself is left
at each corner. The dogs

know it and try to help,
nipping at my feet to speed me up, snarling

my path into wider, aching circles.
The best pain's private

though: shades drawn, the radio blaring,
a blanket for a mat and furniture

my only audience.
At times we long to be small and frail,

for someone to feel we are worth
more hurt. So we let

the ribs show, the cheekbones
pushing out from beneath the skin

like ridges on a stone to tempt sculptors.
I knew a woman, once, who loved

to touch my sharp, protruding hip-bone points—
the tips of the *innominate,* she said,

meaning: *nameless.*
She writes sometimes and never fails

to mention some man's gaunt face, a linear
fragility she's drawn to.

Do we exercise for strength, or the pain
that's addictive, those repetitions

of loss we never catch up with?
It doesn't get any easier.

Homage to C. P. Cavafy

From the first evening we met,
I knew I'd fallen, unredemptively, in love,
becoming, in the next few months,
chronically sick with longing,
unable to sleep without first constructing
elaborate courtship fantasies
in which his sculpted, unblemished face
appeared at my door, lips parted.
What's worse, we became friends.

Charming, solicitous, a neurasthenic,
he hated to be touched, even in private,
disliked being seen shirtless,
drank pots of coffee
to keep his nerves on edge.
He called me the only one in the city—
besides his psychiatrist—to whom he could speak.
And because of this, he explained,
we should never, could never, go to bed.

Often we'd meet for long walks,
stopping by the river to watch the rowing teams,
their boats with those thin oars
skimming the surface like water striders.
Sometimes he spoke of the tortured affair
to which he and an eminent physicist
were habitually attached. Then I'd stretch
beside him and raise one hip,
striking a pose I hoped seductive.
Or else I'd try to maneuver these talks

to our deepening friendship, to the notion
that two such intimate minds
should naturally merge their bodies.

He would remark how the late-afternoon sun
struck the factory windows on the far bank,
making the building appear lit, or ablaze, within.

The Paradise Cafe

As though a train weaved under me,
my legs quaver as I stand, won't yield
to grace. No risk in this paradise,
just accidents, the orbits of eyes.
Through the red and scented haze
I drift as one possible body, a random
choice of looks. Studied in beauty or exile,
faces stare back as if from a story
where desire is the premise
with no development, just detail:
tongue-shaped stains on a table,
seductive talk suspended
with a kiss, occasional tattoos.
Later we might rise and leave
a coil of sheets, too weary
in their dawn embrace to come;
or a leg might lie across mine
and remain awhile, allowed
to travel past the body's
single edge of need.
But here if we don't stand,
we dance in place, glancing
the muscular problem of desire,
which like the skin does not age well,
betrays us when we speak of it.
I could choose you, or you, or you,
or watch you meet another, the neon sheen
enlivening your gifted smiles, your eyes
favored for a moment in that light.

Provincetown, October

We can picture the land's gesture, how it reaches
        into water, curls back, a broad-bladed
curved sword, or just another muscular recoiling.
        That's why our landlord framed this map
tattooed with roads and county lines.
        But the real body of the land—
dunes the wind shapes into burnished chests,
        eelgrass flourishing in shallows—
we must discover for ourselves.

        You've gone walking. Watching this map,
askew against our cottage's knotted wall,
        an ancient heater chuffing its warm column
to the roof, I feel October in my hands,
        counting on my thumbs the faces
leaving us behind: the jewelry store owner,
        his hands and ears a ritual of rings,
who closed his shop before we guessed his age;
        the jewel-eyed waiter you paid too much
attention to, who's hitching south
        "to find a company, perfect the dance."

Yesterday we scouted the Cape's edge,
        the beachline sloping to a snow-capped sea;
then prowled around *Land's End,* the last hotel,
        whose literal-minded name seems useful now,
a sign worth stealing, to make my case
        for losses the world imposes, then refines:
sand dispelled into ocean, ocean into sky,
        or the pitch pine marketplace for sex

made poor now by the cooling air
　　until there's no one new to embrace.

Then you return, breathlessly narrating
　　how you left a page of notes in a cafe,
dialogue you jotted from its last day
　　then tucked beneath your saucer with the tip.
When the waiter finds it, he may hear
　　his own voice verified, softening perhaps
the noise of endings in the air, each dune
　　swept clean of eros and heroes,
as winter unpacks, finds vacancies, settles in.

Garlic

Spicing the close
air of the staircase—
a familial smell.
I wake to its flavor
as if I'd picked it
myself: ganglioid bulb,
veined brittle skin,
the flesh that sweats
and makes the lazy
nervy, like the Romans
who believed its oil
cured sloth in slaves.
Maybe it's the look
that stimulates:
buttocks in husks,
tightly wrapped
underground package;
perhaps its aftertaste
penetrating fingers
for days, indelible
piquancy, a whiff
of pungent memory . . .
How susceptible
we are!, how sure
of the sugary
cures of the past—
the whistle downstairs,
the steam iron's
breath on our faces,
till even the tinge
of ammonia from wet

bedsheets is a childhood
serving us notice.
I open my eyes
and the moon's a sliced
clove in blue broth.
Bitter-tongued,
I could mourn all
I've lost a taste of;
but between now and then,
someone else's simmering
privacy rises,
four flights down.

Maps

Do we love them for their honesty,
for the good faith of their place names,
or because the town lines strike us

sadly, as boundaries must?
Driving from Ice Valley to Cranberry Hill,
we were here. And here. And here.

I don't remember much of either,
but there was nothing like the pleasure
of watching you unfold our map

and smooth it out in the dashlight,
pressing it across your lap like fabric.
I'd lost track too, worked hard to steer

the curves that bore no likeness to our bodies,
terrains so strange to us that day,
we didn't have a clue where we were heading. . . .

But maps remind us we have taken place,
and maps don't exaggerate, won't make claims
to satisfy our craving for a state

where everything we want stays put,
and best of all they're difficult
to fold away once opened. Love,

with all we'll learn about erosion,
let's keep a map between us, or better yet
a globe. Who wouldn't want to grasp the world?

We can close our eyes and point,
our fingertips picking up the dust
from the continents, the Indian Ocean:

briefly we'll look like children, or gods,
squatting above the earth we've spun and blurred,
homeless until we stop it with our touch.

Poem from a Balcony

Tonight the stars pulse and there is no moon,
and our evening meal's a memory.
Traffic swarms and dissipates below—
not regular, but rhythmical enough
to take its place in nature.
The woman I live with and overhear
undresses: not for me or sleep,
but for the comfort nakedness supplies.
As I sense her body's motions
in the room behind me, her beauty,
my desire, seem approximate,
close but inexact. So I read
patience into the blinking traffic lights—
in the jeweled, urban night
they keep directing, halting cars
long since disappeared. For a moment
I'm convinced we are protected, held
within the smaller patterns of survival:
drapes recording a late-August breeze
too slight to feel, the accidental
human postures of our scattered clothes.
Often I have felt them witness us.
Inhumanly tranquil, the city's my accomplice
in distraction, will not come to rest before
my eyes. I turn from it toward you.

Head of a Young Girl

Vermeer

How long it must have taken to arrange
her knotted turban, the exact slope of her shoulder,
her face adrift in a vacuum of black space;
and that startled look, as if I'd just touched her
lightly, teasingly, on the nape of her neck,
and then, too late, realized my mistake.
Her eyes round out like the red mound
of her lower lip; her face circles toward me
and away. All morning since you left,
I've tried to get this right.

                         She's the type
to notice and think too much about
all night, like searching for a phrase
I'll never find: how to describe her turban
halving, then pressing back, her left ear?
Is it made of one or separate swathes of cloth?—
the blue wound like a bandage round her forehead,
the gold gathered at the crown but spilling down
to the untouchable spot between her shoulder blades.
"Relinquish, urge, relinquish"—that's what these yards
of silk seem to say, and then take back, unlike
her lips, which simply part to breathe.

It's like naming my favorite parts of your body
when in bed or, when we talk, pointing out inflections
I like best. How difficult to love with the eyes
closed, the mouth shut, how hard to let the perfect

artifacts of desire be. I want the veil of sweat
along your arm more than the arm itself; I admire
your earrings abandoned by the bedside
for their shine, not for the scent
they leave of you.

                    So I go back to noticing
the enormous tear-drop of her earring, how it once
reflected her first audience, Vermeer, tempting me
to peer even closer, as though to see myself.
Naturally I can't, any more than Vermeer would dare
include himself. But suddenly everything I see
rhymes: tear-shaped pearl and pearl-shaped eyes,
curve of her forehead casting back the light
the way a planet reflects the sun, the red
pulsation of her parted lips. She holds me
at arm's length.

                    Loitering in a bookstore once,
I caught her staring from a rack of cards,
her glance unnerving, like a former lover's.
I pictured myself the one man in the crowd
to buy her back from the lust and cruelty
of the marketplace, and she'd recover overnight
her lost inheritance, her high-born roots,
and out of gratefulness consent to marry.
I bought the card but don't remember who
I'd meant it for.

                    This morning I write to you
about a face I've loved from afar too long,

when all the time it's the black background
I care for and stare at, while she stares back,
as if to bid me walk with her, into the dark,
into whatever she grows out of and returns to;
and isn't this the way I look at you—
no more than a yard of air between us,
across the inevitable space between people
learning to face what they want?

Pentimento

They appear gradually as arguments:
this curve of a hand, this single eye

peering through the acceptable landscape.
Could we want them to belong?

We've grown used to the signature
scrawled in one corner, among groves

of fruit trees and thatched huts
assembled in rows, as if the present

rested in contentment, without shading,
distinct as primary color. So it's hard

to believe what was buried
will not remain buried. As the past

sees through us, its shapes
introduce themselves, demanding response:

lines on the hand extend into the branches
of a tree; the eye takes on the grass

as its lashes. Until our world is no longer
simple, but speechless. It's time we spoke:

You've been gone awhile, but that's over,
and we move closer, curious and afraid.

III

An Afternoon in the Afterlife

In the patio of heaven,
they tip their glasses back
and drain them: rainbow
cordials, *goldwasser*. And beyond

the latticework wall, trimmed
with clematis and flax, bicycles
circle, click and purr.
The gardener's left a hose running.

Should we honor them, seeing them
so calm, so guiltless? One scarlet
tanager swoops down, doesn't land,
and its call—*keep back, keep back*—

is so toneless it blends
into their own conversation.
Our suburban departed!—they speak
with a child's whisper, the women

in blue bathrobes, as are the men,
though it's late afternoon—lawn
mowers drone and the trellis bends
cross-hatched shadows toward their feet.

The Daredevils of Flood's Hill

The summer I was five,
I listened to their cavalry of shrieks,
as sullen afternoons they hurtled down
the steep, seductive hill:
the older boys on sleek Schwinns,
the young ones following
on thick-tired bikes,
basketed, inelegant, resistant.

Curfewed in my yard,
I watched them jostle and brag
at the hill's crest, gathering
speed and fanning out
into their downhill charge,
the closest thing
to weightlessness their bodies knew.

And always the one boy
who'd fail to skirt the hollowed-out
depression halfway down,
whose bike spun up, inscribing
an arc against the resonant air,
before it landed
on his breathless, earthbound figure.

Then the ambulance,
its first note slurring
to a high whine, magnified his cries,
like memory, seeking injury, something to mourn.

My Accomplished Friend

The neighbor's kids are torturing a trumpet,
drawing out to breaking point just one
slack note—a sound so genuinely awful,
from the start I knew its source was human.
I'm impressed by their persistence: three weeks
and not one melody.
                            For a month
in grammar school I tried the clarinet.
My hump-backed tutor spat into a reed
until his cheeks took on that glazed look
of polished fruit. "Music is our purest
form of art," he said, "it makes no claims
to meaning." I agreed and gave it up,
but always watched my more accomplished friend
pump out his onetwo onetwo clarinet drills
as if they were the sentence for my failure.

Now I wonder if the mind elects to hate
those things it can't embrace. Some days
I pummeled that poor dwarf I called my friend
near the railroad where we drilled with hands for oil.
His sparrow fingers scrambled through the dirt
until I couldn't stand it, pushed his face,
again and again, into our shallow trench.
Let him stay there till he dies, I thought—
who'd notice?
                            Not that burned-out school, for all
I know long since pulled down, not these kids
for whom an endless whine's enough. They play on
as though the trumpet's cry might find its way,
with no one's help or talent, into music.

The Youngest Son

The stereo plays "Victory at Sea,"
the heath-kit stereo my father bought
and built all wrong himself. And I lie
on the rug beside him, while the fire
shoots black chestnuts against the screen,
the chestnuts we tossed in, savoring
their small explosions. My unshaven father
leaning back to think of naval battles,
his face at ease in a winter I remember.

Upstairs he read his war books privately,
fell asleep before the T.V. screen.
This was his dream: four missions in a row
he flies without charts, without a crew.
When the flak starts he's alone above the ocean,
no ship in sight. His target is a raft
from which his son lobs chestnuts into the sea.
They explode like depth charges. Angry,
he zeros in, goes down.

                    Someone must speak
for the youngest son, whose name is Steven,
Steven named to even out the family.
There's the back staircase where he hides,
feels the varnish soften beneath his heels.
He builds his fort in a maple tree,
he sometimes sits on his father's lap
and drives the car, and from his room

a record crackles on the phonograph—
Music-to-Tie-Your-Shoes-by; Music-from-under-
             the-Sea.

Once I woke up in a fever, my head
weighted to the three-fold stack of pillows.
I could hear my father shouting *run it off!*
In the Air Force there's no place for sickness,
they just run it off. After twenty years,
the fever's still in the palm of my hand,
my hand holding and shaking his, the hand
that once would press against his stubbled chin
and rub for friction, scouring that face.

Manasquan

Pulling up sharp beside the cottage
where we summered all July, as I
peered out the green, screened-in porch,
my father always arrived on Friday, 5:15,
gunned the engine once. His damp jacket
tucked beneath an arm, his hat
and briefcase shelved above the dash,
he pulled the screen door shut
carefully, kissed my mother twice
and grabbed a towel.

        And always I'd wait
outside the bathroom, pressing my ear
against the door to hear him change—
a hushed sound as he folded his clothes.
And always I'd tag behind him to the beach,
the sand that stung my feet all afternoon
now a tepid, grainy feeling on my soles.
He jogged in place, touched his toes,
I listened to the repetitions of his breath.

There were rules to his routine
a boy could not explain, although I knew
the ocean was a solvent to dissolve
another week of thankless work,
and its undertow could wash away
that figure who'd march in anger,
speechless, from my room, if it wanted to.
But my father also thanked the sea's resemblance—
how it labors night and day but never tires—

while he sought its otherness, all its notions
foreign to ambition.

     Every Friday evening,
six o'clock, high or low tide,
my father waded past the breakers.
Waist-deep, he let his arms swing loose,
then churned the water to a froth
and slapped the brine against his chest.
And when he saw a swell loom up,
perfect by some private measurement,
he joined his hands, lunged out.
His red trunks flashed for a second.
He leveled out with two strong kicks.
I watched the water take him in.

Thirty-Three and a Third

He plays a record from his past.
It goes round and round:

Sunlight through a blue curtain,
and relatives coming in
to pile their coats on a rack.

Tell them to be careful,
his mother says,
at the base the wood is split.

He hears an uncle whispering
as if in grief for someone dead.

Or else it's the drone of the clock
that runs on sunlight, the clock
slowed with the curtain shut.

He'd like to hear something else—
that aria his mother sang
off-key each morning;

the brittle cough of his sister
as she called out in sleep
from the bed next to his.

As he remembers he listens
to the record go around.

He dreams he's in danger of sinking
into the record, into the speakers.

Reaching for his wife,
he feels the bed go around,

while cars turn past his house,
and headlights turn round his room,
and the moon passes over them.

He feels as if his body
were covered with black moss,

the kind of blackness he remembers
coming into his room
after all the relatives left,

covering his bed, covering his body
until he forces his eyes open.

All he can see now
is the black vinyl of the record
turning the way the doorknob turned

on his bedroom door.
Whoever entered his room
grieved as if for someone dead.

He won't remember how
he knows this, or who it was.

Mercy

My mother had a knack for healing birds.
The broken legs of starlings, a sparrow's wing,
even a cardinal snatched from our collie's jaws—
she'd coax them all back to life. Her remedy
was mashed bananas mixed with scalded milk.
Each spring the house reeked of that elixir.
She forced it into their mouths with an eye
dropper, until they couldn't be contained
and fled the perch of her outstretched hand.

How astonishing to know I placed my head
against that woman's breast, always falling
from an oak into her arms or bringing her
my skinned and bloodied knees. To remember
is to tour our own banishment, like picturing
shelter in the houses we pass and point to,
the ones with kite string tangled in the trees,
propeller leaves littering the driveways,
children who call from behind walled gardens.

But what I remember most is mother
knocked down and twisted on the kitchen floor,
legs buckled underneath her, skirt and apron
blooming like a sunflower on the tiles.
My father stands above her, in his hand
. . . what? A plate? Nothing but the threat
of his flat palm again? The picture
dissolves into the wash of all that weeping,
like the time I saw her crying in our backyard

when she found a robin well past help.
She held the bird's limp body in her palm—
a folded, rust-stained handkerchief. . . .

Sometimes when I wake, my recent past
fled like the air punched out of my chest,
I'm that boy again who's forgotten where he hid
some necessary charm, a small blue chain
whose metal feel he knows so well, nothing
can hurt him on the way to school. No matter
how I picture mercy as a woman nursing
wounded birds, that boy cannot escape—
the one who stands, helpless, at the kitchen door,
the one who digs holes near the patio, who watches
a survivor swoop down, land on mother's shoulder,
as she probes her garden for the newly fallen.

Thanksgiving

Light ripens across my father's woods,
across my window's backyard view.

"Your mother and I have fixed
your old room up for you," he says—

cardtable desk, ashtray, pen,
so I can memorize again

portions of autumn sun the trees
shine back, lapidary, cold.

And I can hear the eddies of talk
lap against the wall, carrying

back those late-night monologues
from the living room, swells

of applause, brash commercials
keeping me awake past one,

when my father, manic, couldn't sleep
for weeks. Now he's calling me

to point out a purple finch
chipping from the paddock edged

by the row of adolescent pines . . .
but no, that's not quite right:

this year they're tall enough to hide
the neighbor's yard. My father waited

their lifetime for privacy.
"The back forty," he would call

his acre of sunlit birchbark
curling, shedding another year.

We sweep out the garage. He bends,
cursing, to flick a leaf-stem

from the hood of his El Dorado,
spreads out on the gravel driveway

two rakes, two brooms, pruning shears.
"Great minds think alike, and so

do fools," he says, strangely. Then:
"I'll get this place fixed up before I die."

Freud's Desk, Vienna, 1938

The little gods and demons fall
in across your desk like infantry—
Egyptian, Greek, Etruscan toys
spanning two millennia. Some wear hats

with wings, others horned helmets:
athletic satyrs, jackal-headed women
standing uniformly muscular, satisfied
they have outlived the centuries.

How would you have analyzed the movie
monsters I adored? I glued their limbs
together, daubed their lips with rivulets
of blood, and took them into bed:

a goblin-child's desire to join
"the living dead," then rise again
to take revenge against his makers?
You said a monstrous infant survives

inside us, although a grandchild
to you resembled an oriental doll—
*the youngest but most precious piece
of my Chinese collection.* . . . I try to read

the blurred spines behind your warriors.
Maybe they're your own regiments,
the artillery you used on us,
leaving our loves, our childhoods,

and our love of childhood
like torched Victorian houses.
Maybe the resistance has slipped in,
a fifth-column of patricidal spies.

One year past this picture,
nearly speechless with cancer,
your once-faithful followers now
murderous sons and daughters, you kept

a list: the eight worst mutineers.
But this spearhead of devils and gods
never broke rank. Forced to London,
you redeployed them on your desk

as if their order, a visitor remarked,
took part in some vast reconstruction.
Yet the child you exposed in us
is selfish, disorderly, endlessly plays

games of war. Is it enough
to resurrect that little creature
we know by heart? *Everything's here,*
you told your visitor, *only I'm not here.*

Letter from Boston, Patriot's Day

You've asked for news, the certain
diminishment of fathers. Alive
or newly dead they'll always move us
one year farther from them.
                        You've told me
much of yours—the one to whom music
meant everything, the one who left you
resemblances in the lives of famous men:
Gauguin stranding his family, Brady's soldiers
wanting to be held.
                        As I write,
the citizens march through our streets
in redcoats, bluecoats, white belts
X'd across their chests, their muskets
waking the massacred to praise them back.
We prefer the lesser cruelties
of the personal.
                        Though we rarely call
them that, we call them back: the woman
your father left with you, the way
my hands tremble when I greet my own.
When you visit this city that can't give up
its past for anything, let's mention these
quietly, events among others spoken of,
because our fathers are resting
and shouldn't be disturbed.

Ailanthus

Short-lived tree of heaven,
expatriate outside my window,
just today I learned your name.
For years you gathered the sea's
lathery fog into your branches,
having drawn the mist inland
and threaded it between
your lance-shaped leaves.
I'd never known trees
had such gifts, could hold
a sense of what the ocean
gives and takes: the green
pages of seaweed, inky
silt from riverbanks—
all the curious
detritus of a world I let
slip by.
       So I'll question
this traveler from China,
exiled here as nourishment
for silkworms, and carefully
I'll learn if knowledge survives
in any soil, backyard, before
it's stripped by insects, salt.
And if we can't name paradise
but just these so-called earthly
versions (this *Ailanthus,*
aging, cracked and striped,
darkening in rain), each day
the world still grows a little
less anonymous.

"Marie's Snow": for Marie Howe.

Several lines in "Uncle in Sunshine" were suggested by passages scattered through the work of Wallace Stevens.

"The Narcissus": for Leonard Gill and Sarah Saint-Onge.

A few of the lines in "To Francis Jammes" were adapted from passages in his work.

"Provincetown, October": For George Knuepfel.

"Head of a Young Girl" owes a debt to Edward Snow's book, *A Study of Vermeer*.

Some of the information in "Freud's Desk, Vienna, 1938" is derived from *Freud and His Followers*, by Paul Roazen.

"Letter from Boston, Patriot's Day": for Ira Sadoff.

"Ailanthus": for Stephen Tapscott.

Photo by Michael P. McLaughlin

Steven Cramer was born in Orange, New Jersey in 1953. Since receiving his MFA from the University of Iowa in 1978, Mr. Cramer has worked as an editor and has taught writing at M.I.T. and Boston University. In 1983, Mr. Cramer received a fellowship from the Artists Foundation of the Massachusetts Council on the Arts and Humanities, and in 1984 he was awarded a grant from the National Endowment for the Arts. He lives in Cambridge, Massachusetts.

OTHER GALILEO BOOKS

The Four Wheel Drive Quartet, a fiction by Robert Day
New World Architecture, poetry by Matthew Graham
The Maze, poetry by Mick Fedullo
Keeping Still, Mountain, poetry by John Engman
On My Being Dead and Other Stories, by
        L. W. Michaelson
The Intelligent Traveler's Guide to Chiribosco, a novella
        by Jonathan Penner